Confessions of a Catechist

Confessions of a Catechist

by LAWRENCE CASTAGNOLA, S.J.

DIVISION OF THE SOCIETY OF ST. PAUL

alba house
STATEN ISLAND, N.Y. 10314

Nihil Obstat:
    Raymond T. Powers, S.T.D.
    Censor Librorum

Imprimatur:
    Joseph P. O'Brien, S.T.D.
    Vicar General, Archdiocese of New York
    March 2, 1970

The nihil obstat and imprimatur are official declarations that a book or pamphlet is free of doctrinal or moral error. No implication is contained therein that those who have granted the nihil obstat and imprimatur agree with the contents, opinions or statements expressed.

Library of Congress Catalog Card Number: 71-117201

SBN: 8189-0181-0

In grateful memory of my grandparents.

Contents

Introduction

"It seems there has been a failure in communications." This sentence sums up the dilemma of our modern era — the so-called age of communication. Parents are at a loss in understanding their children. Catechists cannot rely on traditional formulae to communicate the truths of religion. The new attitudes towards war and peace, race and non-violence, women and the Church's mission leave many adults in a state of confusion. And they look to the Church for guidance and encouragement.

These chapters were written for that parent or catechist who is trying to gain a better knowledge of today's youth and the problems of communication not only between parent and child but also between the Church and the world.

I wish to thank the editors of *Pastoral Life Magazine* who encouraged this publication.

Chapter 1

A View of Teenagers and Adults

As a field worker in the jungle of adolescence, I am humored by the psychological editorializing which portrays today's teenagers as idealistic, involved, willing to take risks and altruistic. And, of course, Johnny's virtues are in stark contrast to his parents' non-involvement, traditionalism, personal restraint, desire for security, status consciousness and unwillingness to take risks for justice. Sorry, I'm an agnostic. I don't believe in the "good news" proclaimed by the evangelists of adolescence. My perception tells me most teenagers will settle for the values of their parents in one form or another. And when the rhetoric of justice and brotherhood fades out, about 10% will remain to do the real work. If my judgment seems harsh, it's not because I am against teenagers. With Johnny there is the possibility of change. There is hope for tomorrow's world — despite adult instability, hypocrisy and lack of leadership. If I have a bone to pick, it is not so much with the journalists who lie about teenagers to sell magazines. It's rather with adults like myself who are afraid of being the teenager's source of stability.

Adolescence is by its very nature a time of confusion. And today we see this "natural" confusion compounded by mixed-up adults (I often wonder why there are not more neurotic teenagers). If you experimentally condition an animal to certain behavioral patterns and then introduce sudden interruptions, certain psychic disorders will result. For example, a normal cat was turned into a neurotic and then an alcoholic simply by giving it a blast of air at the times it was conditioned to expect food. Though Johnny is more complex than his cat, he is not immune from the laws of conditioning. He is brought up to respect certain adults. Even when his parents prove to be unstable, he feels he can count on a priest to be stable. Then, while stepping over the threshold of adolescence, he discovers Father Jones has himself unresolved problems. He may prove to be bitter and unhappy. Or he may suddenly leave the active priesthood. Values Johnny once took for granted now become question marks. "Is it really important to go to Church or even to believe?" Father Jones may be able to give rationalizations for his problem or his leaving, but this doesn't help Johnny's confusion. Teenagers believe in what they see, not in sermons however eloquently preached. One may say that there should be no strict identification between "Church" and "priest." But that's not the way it is. The confused priest is bound to confuse the faith of the young person. Lack of charity in the hierarchy, suspension of priests, marriage of priests — these phenomena exist and Johnny is well aware of them. And when he says to his parents: "I'm not going to Mass;

it's just superstition for old ladies," he might be asking for help. He might be saying, "Help me in my confusion. Show me the way. Give me an example of stability, belief and love."

Johnny was conditioned to respect his parents, pillars of his childhood stability. During his high school years he may come to the realization that his parents are drop-outs from life. He may realize that his Dad has a greater identity problem than he does. Yes, Dad, who gives a weekly sermon on the evils of weed and LSD — the "adolescent's escape" — himself employs a well-rationalized use of alcohol for his escape. So Johnny may turn on. And the journalists say he is "seeking answers to life" while in reality he is avoiding questions and answers just like Dad.

If a teenager doesn't get too lost in his own little world, he may admit he is confused. This is why there is hope for him. Some catechists would rather work with adult groups because they are more manageable, respectful and reverent than teenagers. I personally don't mind putting up with noise, triviality, confusion, four-letter words and iconoclasm from the adolescent world. At least you have a feeling of hope, a feeling that the teenager can still be honest.

The dishonesty of the adult world is harder to take. Their "cool" attitude, better known as "hypocrisy," is more irreverent than Johnny's "the Mass is stupid." Allow me to recount a recent experience of this "cool hypocrisy." A nun who operates a home for dependent girls was shopping for a place to house the teenage brothers of her girls. A home, ideal in price and facilities for the seven boys, was found in an old, seemingly respectable neighborhood. The Knights of Columbus offered to buy the home. The program for the boys was licensed, supervised and tried. But the residents rose in perfect unanimity to exclude them. The city planners backed them. No power on earth could have changed the attitude of the residents. Relying on a primitive instinct of territorial integrity, they bristled at the possibility of invasion. The teenage boy, especially one so "un-middle class" as to not have parents, was a threat to neighborhood security. With pathetic eloquence a resident said, "Our neighborhood has always been considered one of the best in the city. We are proud of our trees." Another resident complained there was a parking problem on the block. The fact that the teenagers didn't own cars was irrelevant. Another complained that allowing a boy's home would open the neighborhood's floodgates to other innovations. A resident with a more logical bent figured that every teenager had at least two friends. Thus on certain nights when all were present, the neighborhood would be over-run. The residents showed appreciation in rhetoric for such a program, but "not in our nice area." None would admit the plain fact that they wouldn't risk the slightest discomfort, that they feared teenagers, that they were irrational. With adults such as these, it's not difficult to understand why Johnny wants to destroy systems even though he can offer no replacements. And if Johnny sees such people going to Church on Sunday, can you wonder why he says Christianity is a joke?

It's obviously false to generalize on the adult world by the kind of example just cited. It's inaccurate to think in stereotypes of "adult" and "adolescent." Some boys I teach are more adult than their parents. Others will probably never reach psychological adulthood. At the risk of seeming to contradict the purpose of this chapter, I find it impossible to generalize on the virtues and vices of adults and adolescents. However, it is possible to do some demythologizing. And for the moment, I'll just pick on youth.

What are the myths surrounding today's teenager? It is said that Johnny is more socially conscious than his parents. It is true that there are more students interested in social issues than years ago. The picket line is deemed more important than the age-honored pantie raid. But one might validly ask: "Why is Johnny on the picket line?" Is he there because his girlfriend is there? If he is black, is he there because he would be called an "Uncle Tom" otherwise? Is he there because a professor told him to be there? Is he there because he simply needs an outlet for his biological aggressiveness? In other words, does he really have convictions for his social activity or is he caught up in the parade spirit? I would say that many of today's youth are concerned about justice in their activism. With many others it is simply an outlet like playing football or chasing a greased pig.

There is another myth about Johnny's openmindedness. While it is generally true that teenagers today do not put people into racial categories, they do have categorical minds. Some are downright medieval. It is not uncommon to see high school students dismiss all of biblical literature (which they haven't even read) with the summary statement: "It's all a bunch of fairy tales." With many, ignorance is never an obstacle to expressing a dogmatic opinion. If these teenagers could only see their own dogmatism in pronouncing on difficult questions such as capital punishment, abortion, pre-marital sex, war and drugs, they might unwillingly clasify themselves as "adults." I don't say this simply to criticize youth. Closemindedness is learned from the adult world.

Psychologists have written about the teenager's search for identity, his need for peer security, his sexual confusion, etc. Johnny has these symptoms. He can drive his pious parents mad by his criticism of Church, nuns and motherhood. But adults have the same symptoms. It's one kind of disrespect for Johnny to say, "O . . . you" after being corrected. But this adolescent disrespect is almost humorous in comparison to the cool variety by residents who exclude others from their neighborhood. There is a certain refreshing aspect to the adolescent hang-up.

Strangely enough, the teenager who thinks he is rebellious and unlike adults really resembles those he rejects. Johnny speaks of dope, sex and rebellion as though they were just discovered by his generation. He can't see that his symbols of emancipation are the very tools employed by the "ugly adult." If Johnny really wanted to get even with adults, he would try something really new — like honesty.

I believe in change and in the future. I believe

that man can evolve into something more than a thing who wages war and cheats others. I believe today's youth has the potential to bring about the reign of justice and brotherhood. But too many of us just wait for results — like an over-flooding of applicants to the Peace Corps or the Lay Volunteers. We can't afford to just sit back and "let it happen." Nothing is going to happen without direction and inspiration. It may be satisfying (in a kind of negative way) to be able to say: "I told you this generation would be no more idealistic than our own." But as soon as we are content with that kind of reflection, the adolescent's criticism of us is justified.

Chapter 2

Confession of a Catechist

Any qualified teacher should be able to describe his course and hand an administrator a copy of his working syllabus. But when you're a high school catechist, the simple question about content and method evokes a dumbfounded expression — like you were asked to explain Einstein and Chardin in one breath. You're more like a quarterback calling audibles on every play. The class situation doesn't allow a neat organized plan to function. And so you borrow from other disciplines despite the criticism: "What does *this* have to do with religion?" One day your class may be reading Plato's *Laws* or arguing the philosophy behind school rules. The next day they may be viewing a film about an anthropologist's experience with chimps or listening to the latest rock sound. To an outsider your course looks like a cry for help, an academic suicide attempt, a neo-Babel. Gone are the textbooks with neat chapter outlines. Student and script have been stuffed into the catechetical test tube. And the experiment is in process. It may explode or prove to be a new discovery. Sometimes you feel guilty for branching out. But you're not convinced that the "tried" is practically true. So you rationalize: "Let him who is successfully teaching high school religion cast the first stone."

In the following paragraphs allow me to slide a few pebbles off the water's surface. Recently while addressing a group of ladies, an anguished parent asked how her daughter could stop attending Sunday Mass while at a Catholic University. When I attempted to give reasons why teenagers in general weren't going to Mass, one lady walked out. She felt a moral imperative to report me to her husband and pastor as though a statement of opinion meant a desire to overthrow the establishment. Her action in a way symbolized some of the mistrust that does surround the high school or college catechist. It's true that little Johnny, now cracking through the shell of parental piety, is often iconoclastic. It's true that his pastor doesn't see him at Sunday Mass. And it's understandable that the question should arise: "What are they teaching him in religion class?" Not having the clearest idea of what is going through Johnny's mind, many think the solution to his impiety is a decisive dispensation of imperatives. But the catechist by his daily association with Johnny sees more deeply into the problem. And he's not willing to postpone Johnny's maturity with more simple solutions, like "if you do (or don't) it's a mortal sin." While my present thoughts may not help anyone to reach Johnny, they may at least serve as a partial apologia for the "catechist in transition."

There are perhaps teachers who have successfully

taught Scripture to high school boys. I haven't. But at least no class staged a Bible-burning ceremony in my honor. Perhaps I'm too intimidated by the plea I get the opening day of school: "Please, anything but the Bible." Such an attitude has forced me to try to put the themes of Scripture in a contemporary context. While a sophomore may find it boring to listen to a parable from *Matthew,* he usually listens to the creative effort of a classmate. And so you help them create. The following is an example of this attempt. Written by a sophomore, it does not remain true to the original. But perhaps Christ would have told one like this today.

" 'I hate this place. All I'm waiting for is to turn eighteen so I can leave. We're not a family, so why should we pretend.'

"In a few days Mora would turn eighteen and be leaving her home for the land of marshmallow skies, where peace and love would reign. She was sick of her parents and her older brother who could 'do no wrong.' So she took the money her parents had put aside for a college education and took off for Denver. She was last seen hitchhiking with some longhair outside of Reno.

"After a few weeks she had her fill of pot and free love, so she decided to go back to her middleclass family in Sacramento. She didn't go back out of love, but simply because she needed medical attention.

"When she returned home she found her mother drunk. Her mother told her how her brother had taken a swing at the old man and had been thrown out of the house. Dad was at work. He worked later and later these day and would only come home for a few hours of rest.

"Mora's mother poured her a drink, and they both sat waiting for Dad to come home, wondering whether he would be happy, angry or even notice Mora's return."

* * *

Besides having no success at exegesis or historical criticism, I confess an abhorrence of textbooks. Every year my syllabus changes, and there is a certain day-to-day uncertainty which accreditors and lovers of stability cannot admire. I use paperbacks like Frankl's *Man's Search For Meaning*, Gregory's *Nigger* or Richard Wright's *Blackboy*. Few of the writings I employ are directly theological. And yet I don't think I am copping out on tradition. The authors of Scripture used current stories to get across an idea. It doesn't seem untraditional to use the current as vehicles of revelation.

I confess playing down an authoritarian approach to truth. When we discuss the soul or the existence of God, it is in terms of the student's experience. At all possible costs I try to avoid "The Church Says." So embedded in the young person's mind is the equation of "Church" with "hierarchy" that it takes ceaseless effort to get across the simple idea that *they* are the Church.

I accuse myself of over-identifying with my students. I never took the advice of those philosophers of education who caution teachers to maintain a professional aloofness. I confess spending more time with teenagers than reading theological journals. It often feels so trivial to have to be where the teenage action is. But I feel my real work is done at a football game or an after-the-game hangout.

It really isn't too difficult to enter the teenager's world. But the problem with so many adults is they would rather talk about Johnny's problem than face him. I remember attending a catechetical convention which devoted two days to the discussion of high school students and their problems of faith. Experts shared their insights on the generation gap, the crisis of faith and other problems of the adolescent world. The closing session of the convention was an experimental Bible Vigil demonstrated by students from local Catholic high schools. About half of the educators who discussed the relevance of the Church to teenagers didn't stay for the service. It turned out to be a creative liturgical innovation employing ballet, and folk music with Scripture. The fact that few stayed to see it symbolized the adult fault — "Let's discuss kids but not spend too much time with them."

I confess failure to do justice to the questions of speculative theology. In a sense I over-react to the polemical approach to religion where a truth is something to be argued. I've found that boys who have "intellectual" difficulties with the faith in their sophomore year have more or less the same difficulties in their senior year. And at the risk of oversimplifying, I find that these intellectual difficulties have complex personal histories. If I take time out to really talk out a boy's problem about the existence of God, I usually find his agnosticism runs deeper than speculative theology. He is usually a boy who has lost trust in most people. And he admits he will have to regain trust in people before he can begin to think of a God who may or may not be trusted. The catechist has to be at least one person he can begin to trust.

I confess playing down the distinction between the sacred and the secular. While I realize there is a danger of reducing Christianity to a kind of humanism, I think there is more danger in presenting a dehumanized Christianity.

As a result of emphasizing the "revelation" contained in much of contemporary experience, I accuse myself of playing down private revelations given to the saints of old.

I accuse myself of having confidence in today's youth. They want answers and direction. They want to be a part of a living Church. But they are confused. After giving a talk recently on the Church at a public high school, a girl remarked, "We feel that the Church has no place for teenagers." I've heard that statement expressed in many ways. And the more, I think about it the more I realize how much work we have to do, how the parish and parents must pick up where the catechist leaves off.

And, I confess having faith in the future and faith in experimentation both in the classrooms and in the liturgy. Once we lose our fear of experimenting (which can be a form of listening), we may start making progress.

Finally, I confess wanting too much sympathy for being a high school religion teacher. It's really not true that religion is the most difficult subject to teach. It's the teenager who is difficult to teach regardless of subject matter. And he is difficult because he wants example.

Chapter 3

Adolescence and Sexual Confusion

Adults tend to forget that teenagers go through the pangs of sexual confusion. They tend to forget their own experience of growing up. They don't understand this confusion and therefore either fear teenagers, shy away from them or consign them to the lower regions of Dante's hell for their lack of morals.

In the midst of their frustration, adults argue over the goodness or badness of sex education in the schools. Some argue that education in the schools will provide the only effective remedy for society's ills: family disillusion, promiscuity, etc. Others argue that the school has no business in an area so personal. It seems that this kind of debate over public education is just a smokescreen adults use to avoid the real issue which has little to do with formal education. I believe there is something the schools can teach — the biological process of reproduction, the sociological effects of the misuse of sex, the basic psychology of sexual differences, the anthropology of family life, etc. This can be helpful — on the condition that teenagers are given something more. And that "something" is an example of tenderness and self-sacrifice in their families. Our culture is so preoccupied with the physical act of sexual intercourse that we have forgotten that ninety-nine percent of married life is another kind of interaction. Parents are giving their children sex education for better or worse whether they realize it or not. If a teenager doesn't grasp the experience of being loved and seeing a self-giving kind of love, what hope is there that he will understand sex as the result of slides, movies, textbooks and lectures?

Yet how many adolescents are brought up in families where they grasp through experience the value of their own persons? How many are loved unselfishly? The pollsters can't answer these questions. I think the adolescent who is promiscuous has a problem more basic than a misuse of his sexual faculties, a problem buried in his own insecurity, his own lack of a self-image. The whole fuss made by certain school boards whether or not to introduce high school courses in sex education often miss the real problem facing the confused adolescent. He or she won't be scandalized by a movie of the birth of a baby. The real burden is to sensitize the young person towards the value and uniqueness of the human person, to give them a realization of the beauty of a relationship in which man shares God's creative power. It should be obvious that the classroom alone can't do this. For a moment let's take a look at two confused high school boys — Bob and John. Their problems are not the same. But both need help in passing through the crisis of adolescence.

Bob is outwardly a well-adjusted senior. He gives everyone a good first impression. His parents are well-respected in the community. Few would suspect that Bob and his parents were in conflict. In early grade school Bob began to think of himself as a ladies' man. He had a quick wit and a pleasant smile which attracted the girls. In the ninth grade he made his first visit to a prostitute at the dare of some older friends. These friends made him feel he was "big and bad," a man. It was apparently a desire to further prove his manhood which led him, without any particular remorse of conscience, to seek conquests among the more lax of his female peers. He really didn't worry about his behavior until the day he received notice from a girl that he was a father.

Bob was afraid. He was afraid for the first time, but he now couldn't cover his anxiety with a smile. His fear was not particularly for the girl or the baby, but for himself. "What's going to happen to me?" was his preoccupying thought. He had no intention of marrying the girl or desire to support the child. His "solution" to the problem was to drink a little more. This "unfortunate mistake" didn't force him to change his basic attitudes toward life. He had no intention of giving up his style. He would simply be "more careful" in the future.

Moralizing with Bob would be fruitless. Punishment, too, will have limited effects. It almost seems necessary that something tragic happen to him, something to shock him from his attitude of complacency. Bob didn't lack intelligence. And he had a basic goodness. But somewhere in his psyche was a bitter sense of failure which sought outlets in sexual conquest. All the best sex education of the schools would not have helped him — unless by sex education one includes therapy for personal problems.

I'm not aware of schools with the machinery to probe such deep-rooted problems. Many boys and girls are like Bob. Sex becomes a weapon of revenge, an outlet for frustrations. A girl tries to get pregnant only to bail out of her home. Another gives herself to boys because she is in desperate need of recognition. Sex becomes a way of acting out for the emotionally starved. School sex education may help, but hardly be a solution for such teenagers.

John's "sex problem" was quite different from Bob's. Whereas Bob wouldn't recognize a true problem, John over-emphasized and magnified a minor problem until it became personally intolerable. John was a straight A student and interested in just about everything. He participated in many school activities from athletics to drama to works of the social apostolate. He would fit any educator's "My Pride and Joy" list. To those who knew him he was the "ideal." But few of his friends suspected that he was a tortured and tormented boy. Few knew of his feelings of frustration, guilt and inadequacy. And the proximate cause of his feelings was that subject few parents and educators are willing to discuss with an adolescent: masturbation.

When John came to me with his guilt and despair, he prefaced his remarks with: "I'm lost, really hopeless." At first I thought his pessimism was a put-on and didn't take him too seriously. He continued: "I don't know why I'm asking for help. You don't have any answers. No one does." Slowly I began to realize his pessimism wasn't a front. After talking out his masturbation guilt, John was still troubled. I asked him to write out the history of his guilt and the different advice given him by confessors. His answer to my request is printed here with his permission.

"Father, before telling you about my experiences in confessionals and counselors' offices, I think it would be helpful to know something about my background. I was never close to my father. Maybe this is the main reason for my problem. As a result of our distance to each other, my father never got around to telling me the facts of life. I discovered them on my own from a 'friend.'

"Later I met another 'friend' who told me how to satisfy my curiosity about sex. That was all there was to it. For the next three years I committed acts of masturbation almost daily until I found out from a book (not my parents) that it wasn't right. I'd had struggles with my conscience before. But the thought that what I was doing could get me to hell was staggering. I knew that I had to tell a priest about it.

"Probably the hardest thing I've ever done was tell my counselor about what was troubling me. It hasn't been any easier to put on paper. My counselor was very understanding. He took the approach of 'buck up, kid, you're not the only one.' He added: 'Just keep confessing it and everything will turn out all right.' His advice was all very nice, very gentle, very encouraging. But it didn't work. I needed a formula. But, as I have discovered, there was and is none.

"Between this session and the next time I was desperate enough to seek a counselor's help, there was a seemingly endless stream of confessions. The closest any of my confessors ever came to helping me was when they didn't try to help me. After confessing self-abuse and not getting a shocked interrogation but only a penance and absolution, I could suppress the nagging feeling of guilt and for a time forget that I was capable of these acts.

"One priest gave me a line about how I should pray to Mary, Queen of Purity, and God would give me all the grace I needed. I'm not trying to cut down the priest's approach. It may have been valid for someone else. But if he had known me, he wouldn't have expected me to rely on God's grace when I don't understand the meaning of God or grace. I haven't found God yet.

"The advice of another priest just about discouraged me from receiving the sacraments — which I've always tried to receive frequently. Confessing to him went something like this:

"I committed self-abuse two . . . ."

"You what?"

"I committed self-abuse . . . ."

"There followed a lecture on how there was 'no reason to commit this sin.' And as if things weren't difficult enough, his voice was like Bill Cosby's impersonation of God threatening to drown-out Noah.

The overtones of hellfire and damnation were clear. After confessing to this priest, I felt so guilty that I needed to forget. And since I don't drink, I took the only road to forgetfulness I knew — self-abuse.

"At that point I was desperate. It had been over a year since I discovered that I would probably go to hell, and I wanted out. I wasn't enough of a coward to commit suicide. So I came to you rather than my original counselor for a conference.

"Our first talk at least accomplished something. It gave me a chance to tell someone closer to my own age and with whom I could identify what had been eating me from the inside for over a year. We established the fact that my acts of masturbation were not condemning me to hell. However, I still felt obligated to confess each act — something which continually became more difficult. The harder it was to confess my sins, the more guilty I felt. The more I felt guilt, the more I thought about it. The more I thought about my problem, the lower my resistance got.

"After your advice my habit got no better. If anything, things took a turn for the worse. In our second session I tried to tell you that I wasn't worried about hell. I told you that I didn't know my own identity, that I couldn't reject a God I knew less about than myself. I told you again that I was bound by a habit I didn't understand. You tried to get me to see the root of my problem is my insecurity. You finally told me not to confess the acts of self-abuse as I described my problem to you. I hope your advice will help."

Some disagree with my approach and the advice given this boy. On the surface it could seem that I was encouraging irresponsibility for personal actions. However, in telling this boy not to confess self-abuse, I was not encouraging moral relativity or preaching original innocence. I felt that in this case the full consent of the will necessary for mortal sin was not present and that confession of the matter was merely increasing John's obsession with the problem. It was the person in front of me who dictated this other approach. And if the case history quoted here has any value, it will be to make adults more sensitive to the individual's personal history — not necessarily to serve as a norm for advice.

John and Bob simply represent two adolescents in sexual crisis. And one can't generalize from these two boys that all teenagers or most have the same kinds of confusion. There are as many varieties of confusion as there are teenagers. John was ready for help and encouragement. Bob gave the impression that he wanted no help, but he too was not the rock which needed no guidance. Too often adults give up with a young person because they see no visible response. It is easy to write off the so-called immoral teenager as hopeless.

Anyone can generalize and philosophize about adolescent sexual confusion, but how many are willing to hand out more than theoretical answers? As Americans we are preoccupied with systems and think we can come up with one to head off venereal disease and premarital pregnancies. The only system I see as feasible is personalism. Parents and educators have to be willing to listen, to understand each other, as well as the confused teenager. But when adults give overwhelming evidence that they are more confused (sexually and otherwise), what can we really expect of youth?

Chapter 4

The Problem of Theological

Communication

There is a kind of religious jargon which we as adults have grown used to but which evokes no pious sentiments in the younger generation. Our use of "churchy" words and phrases may have the same effect on them as some of their music has on the lovers of Beethoven and Bach: "turned off."

So how does a parent or catechist communicate in a day when dictionaries are disregarded? (I have a young friend who uses the adjective "bad" to describe what she considers really good). How does one present concepts of salvation, vocation, authority of Scripture, Mystical Body and Christian love? How does one get through the blockade of words conditioned by history, abused by fanatics and over-used by textbooks?

"Salvation," for example, expresses a central concept of Christianity. But when you use an expression such as "Jesus saves," you invite disaster. "Save" is a word we identify with Blue Chip stamps. And "Jesus saves," has been so plastered on billboards and mouthed by neurotic preachers that its sacredness has been profaned. The whole concept of salvation, being saved, has so smacked of paternalism or a kind of "deus ex machina" rescue that few young people are grabbed by the idea. A young person wants to think in terms of release, freedom and initiative — not being protected or saved. Thus it is the challenge of a teacher to present the *concept* of salvation — which is after all a way of expressing freedom — without using that specific *word*.

Another concept which needs a new vocabulary is the "Christian's vocation to sanctity." The young identify "vocation" with religious life and "sanctity" with the plaster faces they once saw in an Italian national church. Sanctity is always something out of the reach of the ordinary mortal. The pious falsehoods of hagiographers have made it seem that the canonized saints were men and women without faults. Biographies have often glorified masochism as heroic virtue. So if Saint X developed a stiff neck because he never lifted his eyes to the possibilty of seeing a woman, who wants to be a saint? Whether or not we use the word "saint" or "vocation," I believe we have to present the young with examples of virtue they can realistically imitate.

The concept of the Mystical Body is certainly meaningful, beautiful and central to the Gospel. But there has been historically a real problem with the explanation of this phrase. Theologians have tended to try to define membership in the Church. They tried to answer questions such as: "How are Protestants or the non-baptized parts of the Mystical Body?" While this may be an honest theological endeavor, it has devastating effects on the mentality of youth who despise this kind of classification. Because to their minds classification means subordination, saying: "I'm better."

When you tell a young person he should be "another Christ," this too may be a perplexing injunction. How can Henry A strive to be "another" when he doesn't have a hold on his own identity? How can he strive to be another before he even understands himself. One boy expressed his confusion with this injunction in the following terms: "How can I be another Christ, the man totally for others? If I give myself totally to others, am I still a man? Am I to become a machine? And I have so many personal problems, how can I separate myself from them? Jesus is a mystery to me, a total blank. If I am to evolve into him to reach my perfection, I don't want perfection. If I am to be swept into him, I lose my personal significance. Am I worth nothing now as I am with all my imperfections?"

The boy's statement obviously reflects a heretical understanding of "be another Christ," an understanding deduced from religious perfectionism. However if the Pauline injunction to "put on the mind of Christ" is to be presented, it must be done in a way which builds on present human goodness. Christ is not the unreachable, but the one identified with us as we are in our weakness.

There are many other phrases which are ambiguous. One only needs to mention "Christian love." The word love itself is confusing enough to the young without further complicating it. Yet we must use some words to express the realities we believe in. So I guess "love" will have to do for a while.

In criticizing our use of traditional words and phrases I don't mean to imply that the catechetical problem is simply one of semantics. There will always be the basic freedom to accept or reject the Gospel despite the relevancy or irrelevancy of vocabulary. Yet I do think that adults should make a better attempt to communicate the Gospel in a language the young can grasp. Then if the Gospel is rejected, they will at least know what they are rejecting.

The following reflection is that of a senior student who sat at my feet in Religion IV at Jesuit High, Sacramento. It is his analysis of the theological vocabulary problem.

"I've comprised this list of 'hard sayings' entirely from phrases which have given me problems. I've found solutions to most of them, and I included them in the hope that you might be better able to understand what goes on in a fairly average teenager's mind. I hope this helps, because the average high school religion course is badly in need of change, a change that can only be brought about by people who understand what we're thinking.

"GOD: Here is the real problem, the very heart of it. I seriously doubt that most high school students have the right idea, if they have any idea at all, about what a Christian concept of God is. I don't know about other people of my age, but I didn't start resolving my problems with all the apparent contradictions in my religion until I started to think of God in human terms. This might stop a few theologian's hearts, but I don't think it would bother God. After all, people are created in his image.

"HELL: This is a word which, except when I'm trying to express my feelings about a misguided golf shot, really never occurs to me. It used to really bother me, though. I couldn't figure out how God, who is supposed to love the things he creates, could ever condemn a human soul, created in his image, to an eternity away from its creator.

"I've occasionally tried to write poems, and to express my feelings in words. My poems are my image placed in words. No matter how unsightly they might appear to the critical eye, they are a part of me, and I'll never use them for kindling in the fireplace.

"So, if I can't burn my poems, how can God burn souls? My answer is simple enough, I don't think God will condemn anyone to hell eternally. [This is, of course, an erroneous opinion. Christ preached, and the Church has always taught the existence of hell and the fact of eternal damnation (Editor's note).] I do believe however, that all human souls, at one time or another, experience a hell much worse than anything in Dante's torture chamber. It is the indominable aching unrest which has driven men to everything from suicide to overkill. Unrealistic? Idealistic? Perhaps, but I'm content with it.

"FEAR OF THE LORD: Teachers had better start thinking about changing the word 'fear' to 'respect.' If they don't the most polite classification their students will put it in is bull feathers. Any psychologist will tell you that if you go up to someone and say, 'Love me or I'll break every bone in your body,' the only thing you'll get is a superficial response and internal resentment. A God who says, 'Love Me or I'll throw you into hell for all eternity,' could hardly expect more.

"A lot of people may find this hard to believe, but almost all young people really are trying to do what is right. We don't need pithy sayings and trite formulae; we need to be aimed. If you give an explanation for something in terms of human understanding, or the lack of it, we'll probably go along with it. We don't need hellfire and damnation hanging over our heads to do the right thing if we have some understanding of what we're doing and why, but the catechist who expects us to quake in our seats at the mention of God's wrath is likely to receive a good swift kick in his pious truisms and be thrown out on his old testament verbosity. I'm willing to believe that God is capable of destroying me, but I trust him a lot more than I do the man behind the nuclear panic button.

"GRACE: This concept, known among my peers as the Brownie Point System, is sorely in need of revision. Almost any way you phrase it, it comes out sounding like Tinker Bell's stardust or the manufacturer's description of a fireworks display. If a teacher has the temerity to go into the distinction between actual and sanctifying grace, he is likely to be either laughed at or ignored. The average teenager doesn't worry about grace, but when it is mentioned he gets a mental picture of the Baltimore catechism analogy of something which bleaches spotted or black lambs, or sweetens a sour bottle of milk. 'I personally think that black lambs are cute, and I'm fond of sour milk pancakes, so what's God making trouble for?'

"Seriously, though, I do think that the average teenager can understand that God isn't just a detached overseer, but someone who cares enough to want to help. I myself think of grace as a spiritual manifestation of God's love, which is physically visible in such things as the desire to reach out and help others, and the understanding required to undergo physically and emotionally painful situations and still cling to faith and hope.

"SUFFERING IS GOOD: This phrase is a particular problem because it is so easily misunderstood. Most teenagers have seen this theme before in grammar school, in connection with some saint with a name like Rufus of the Great Horned Grebes, who spent his life in total solitude and lived on sea weed and raw fish. With examples like that, it's not too hard to understand why the concept doesn't go over very well. Today's young people want to contribute. I'm not content to withdraw from the world and the people in it, I want to embrace life and fight the world's problems, and if that means getting hurt once in a while, that's all right. I know how to use suffering to strengthen my resolution, and I think that most of my peers understand and accept that. All they need is someone who will take the time to explain that that, and not a hermit's masochism, is the value in suffering. We don't condemn poor Rufus, but whatever his reasoning was, it doesn't agree with ours.

"GOD'S MERCY: The problem here is, I think, a poor choice of words. Mercy is a form of supreme condescension which you feel for someone you are about to obliterate. I don't believe that God or one of his 'angels' * is standing over me with a sort of divine bludgeon, which he refrains from using only at great expense to his vengeful nature. I don't think that this is what a catechist means when he uses the term 'God's Mercy,' but that, to many teenagers, is what he says. If you want to say what you mean, try using 'God's Love.'

"MAN'S FALLEN NATURE: I'm willing to grant that without God, man wouldn't exist, and that without Christ, man would be unworthy to spend eternity in God's presence, but teenagers aren't interested in 'what ifs.' The fact is that man has both God and Christ, and by God's will, man is worthy of God's presence. Young people are only too aware of their shortcomings. What they need is someone who believes in them enough to tell them about their value. Besides, I for one believe that man's value is far more important and far surpasses his 'fallen nature.' I believe that Christ did his job right, and that today's youth can and

---

* Angels may exist, but I'm not going to argue about whether or not they do. The answer would have little bearing on how I am to live my life as a Christian. Until I think that I'm a perfect Christian, I'm not going to worry about the possible existence of an eight-winged super-fairy. (P. S.)

will identify with Christ as a person and an example, if they are brought to the realization that they have in themselves a divine beauty and potential.

"CHRIST; GOD AND MAN: The only problem I see with this is that I never see it any other way. It's always 'Christ; God and man.' You never see 'Christ; God and *Man*' or 'Christ; man and God.' Ninety-nine per cent of the people who call themselves Christians, when asked who Christ is, will automatically reply that he is God, the second person of the Trinity. Ask them where he is, and they'll tell you he sits at the right hand of the Father in Heaven.

"They really do believe in the omnipresence of God, but somehow they picture him as being more in heaven than anywhere else, and he's got Christ right up there with him. Somehow Christ, the man, got lost in the shuffle.

"Tell today's youth to follow Christ, and all they have to go on is a picture of a Supreme Being sitting at the right hand of another Supreme Being in some place whose general direction is "up." It doesn't occur to anyone to stress that Christ has a human body, complete with pain and pleasure, fears and strength, will and emotions, and that he is among us now, in a very real way, in the hearts and minds of all mankind. Christ's divinity is important, but it is also important that he is a man, to whom all of us can relate, and who knows and understands how hard it is to be a man.

"CONTRARY to what most mothers will tell you, the stomach is not the only way to the heart of a teenager. Fortunately for catechists, not usually endowed with talent in the culinary art, there is another path, through the intellect. It can only be traversed by someone ready to give honest, personal answers to questions concerning the basic foundations of the faith. Young people are not nearly so interested in what the Church says as they are in what the people they respect believe. This means that the primary duty of the catechist is to be a Christian and a friend, who is willing not only to explain what the law is, but to answer honestly the question, 'How do you feel about this?' "

Paul Sidenblad

Chapter 5

Adult Christian Racism

If psychologists are correct in saying that the familiar should be treated as unfamiliar, I feel justified in adding this reflection to the analysis of racial prejudice. And I fully realize that any discussion of this topic runs the risk of just adding another page to the prodigious junkpile of brotherhood sermons.

Even if we personally feel no prejudice, something should bother us American Catholics. Many people in our society think we are prejudiced. A research psychologist tells us that some of the most bigoted Catholics are faithful Mass-goers. A sociologist tells us that the Church perpetuates obscurity about race by leaving important things unsaid. A theologian claims that the Church does little to counter a sense of racist exclusivism so condemned by Christ and the Prophets. Our Black Catholic clergymen tell us that our white institution is racist. It seems that any intelligent person would listen to this weight of criticism and examine the rightness or wrongness of his own attitude. Is the "average Catholic" infected with racism — and to what degree?

I should search my own house first. I like to think

of myself as open-minded. Yet I know that I grew up with all my white ghetto friends subtly aware that "Negroes were different." The segregated society I lived in taught me to feel uneasy at the sight of a Black man walking hand in hand with a White girl. I was never formally taught that it was wrong for the races to mix. But there was a kind of unspoken rule. The Negro was the mysterious one. He was the one who might harm you if you got too close. So you didn't even think of going through his neighborhood or fraternizing.

My earliest remembrance of the "other race" was filled with mystery and fear. I was about ten years old and attending a summer camp. A group of young Black boys and girls passed our campgrounds. A boy in our group yelled some racist word which I can't now remember. The Blacks just kept walking and didn't say anything. Five minutes later the boys from the group came back and began to throw rocks at us. I remember a jacknife landing about ten feet from me. As things began to look bad, our camp counselor came running down wielding a baseball bat like a caveman. The kids scattered.

I'll never forget that incident. And to this day I can't decide who was more at fault — the kid with the racist epithets or the counselor with the baseball bat. At any rate the incident symbolizes for me the nature of the problem — lack of communication, fear and irrational retaliation.

It isn't difficult to understand the racism of a child. He's usually imitating an adult. But what of those who should be old enough to perceive a personality behind a color of skin? And what about these adults when they claim to be Christian? For the moment allow me to indulge in the analysis of a Church-going Catholic who is hardly aware of her prejudice, a woman with the accepted kind of non-violent prejudice. She doesn't throw bombs at Negro churches, nor does she applaud those who would do such a thing. She is a good person in her own way, but she never understood Christ.

Mrs. Marjorie X and her sister are all upper-middle-class, white college-educated, practicing Catholics. They are emotionally stable, socially active and reasonable people. The day after Dr. King's funeral, Mrs. X's son made these observations: "My mother claims she's not prejudiced, but she doesn't want to have a Negro neighbor (unless you resurrect Nat King Cole — she loves his voice). She says she would be civil and polite to Blacks. But invite one to dinner? Afraid not. She is proud of the fact that she voted against Fair Housing.

"Now I can understand my Mother's fear of Blacks moving in next door, because she's never known one. I can't understand the reaction of my aunt the day Martin Luther King was shot. While saying it was 'too bad' he was shot, she immediately complained of the flag being flown at half-mast. They could concede he was a great Negro, but not a great American. And all during the day she made statements like: 'King was responsible for riots by preaching civil disobedience,' or 'Why do we praise a man who was often thrown in jail?' She knew nothing about his dedication to higher laws, his non-violence. But I must admit her attitude changed a little after she watched the funeral on TV. She kept repeating: 'We didn't realize how important he was.' Now that last statement seems to be the key to the attitude of my mother and aunt. They are not so much prejudiced as uninformed. They've never seen a ghetto. So they just take a problem and idealize it and give it an oversimplified solution. I don't blame my mother or her sister for their backwardness. It's part of the "white propaganda" that no one, including the Church, has up to this time challenged. My mother didn't even know before his funeral that King was a minister or a learned man. My mother doesn't hate, and yet she asked an irrelevant question like, 'Where did King get the money to travel?' while he lay dead from an assassin's bullet."

This young boy's testimonial hits a sore point few want to recognize. Many of us realize that we haven't challenged the Marjorie X's because they were too influential. Perhaps we feared their slander campaigns or their ultimate threat: "I will go to another church." We have perpetuated a cult of ignorance. I personally haven't forgotten statements I overheard the day of King's funeral. I was naive about the amount of racism that exists in some "Christian" hearts. I overheard a religious say that too much attention was being given a "nigger." I overheard a schoolboy say Negroes were unequal by nature and would never be equal. I heard an "adult" complain of King's funeral delaying openers of major league baseball. With some I sensed an unwillingness to make any positive comment about King for fear of seeming to approve Civil Rights which, in turn, meant "one might move in next to you," or "one might want to marry my daughter." The attitudes I saw crystallize that day told me that brotherhood is only a pious cliché for many Christians.

In speaking of a "white Christian attitude," one risks oversimplifying. No one knows whether Marjorie X symbolizes a majority or minority attitude. People keep their racial thinking to themselves. Yet it is safe to say a great number of respectable and intelligent Christians are credulous about blackness and boot-straps, self-help and handouts, crime and cranial capa-city, civil disobedience and Americanism. The same person who is shocked by a militant's statement — "the flag is a rag" — will smile at the little old lady in tennis shoes who waves a flag for Wallace. This same person will declare, "We have lifted ourselves up by our boot-straps," and fail to realize some minorities don't have any boots. This person will take pride in the fact that his ancestors worked for their status in society and fail to realize one can't sell bananas on streetcorners in today's world. Such a person is ripe for the hysteria of blockbusting realtors. Bombarded with myths from all sides, he doesn't know how to think about race. And in the midst of mass confusion, he becomes simple prey for the black or white extremist and his message of hate.

Extremism (black or white) is not the main issue. It is rather our apathy in neglecting to educate each other on race or challenge folk-ways. It is a preoccupa-tion with "not disturbing people" which is really the disturbing thing. Minorities don't expect us to paint their ghettoes. They don't expect to see me in their churches or neighborhoods giving a witness of friendship. But they wonder why we can't change "white attitudes," why a particular teenager with twelve years of Catholic education still uses words like "nigger" or "jig." They wonder why a religion which preaches "love your enemies" doesn't even recognize the psychological principle of "love or perish." They stand in amazement while the biased Catholic spiritually roasts himself in the flames of his own ignorance.

We can preach on race relations, join marches, sign petitions, lock arms and sing, "We Shall Overcome." This isn't a complete waste of effort. Yet something more is expected from us if we are to change the conclusion of the National Advisory Commission on Civil Disorders: "Our nation is moving towards two societies, one black, one white — separate and unequal." But what is this "something more?" Sorry, there's no easy answer. Most of the necessary legislation has been passed. The problem is with people — always stubborn creatures. How do we get an idea across to Mrs. X — like approval of a minority member living in her neighborhood or working in her middle-class department stores? Perhaps we have a few steps to take before we do any witch-hunting of Marjorie X's. What about bigotry in the priesthood? It exists, but it is kept hidden pretty well. What about our nationalistic thinking — the second cousin of racism? Surely, it's not dead. Many of the whites in large cities are Catholics. And even those who don't throw rocks at civil rights marchers are far from understanding the theology of the vine and branches. Our past wisdom of encouraging "national churches" may be questioned — just as I question the intelligence of a national Catholic church which at this writing offers free pizza to lure a diaspora to retain their national identity. Though patriotism and nationalism are not necessarily racism, they do easily degenerate into superiority thinking. How many of us still subscribe to the colloquial myths — "Spaniards are hot-headed," "Italians are lovers," "Germans are born-scientists," "Englishmen are coldblooded," "Irish are illogical," "Indians are apathetic," "Negroes are physical," and so on. Remnants of the "Nordic Superiority Myth" so utterly disproven by the Nazi prison camps still linger in our collective mentality. We speak of "crossing blood" and are very unscientific when we get on the subject of intermarriage. The myths multiply. We should try to prove that Christianity is not just another myth. Maybe we should concentrate on opening our neighborhoods and schools instead of simply "our hearts."

Chapter 6

The Vocation of Fatherhood

A fundamentalist Christian once reprimanded me for my presumptiousness in allowing others to address me as "father." He quoted the verse from the New Testament: ". . . and call no one on earth your Father, for one is your Father who is in heaven." I dismissed his interpretation of Scripture as childish and unscientific, but later gave his complaint some thought. After all, the saying is attributed to Christ. There must be some meaning to the warning about titles.

While I still allow myself to be called "Father" by those who wish, I can see why some object to the title. There are men in the priesthood, as well as heads of families, who misuse authority. There are men in both vocations who have little or no sensitivity towards the young. They may be biological parents or ordained ministers, but they do not reflect God's fatherhood. To call a vindictive priest or parent "father" is a kind of blasphemy if one comes to understand or imagine God's fatherhood as being similar.

Today's world has a basic problem with fatherhood. Or one might better express the problem by saying the world has a basic problem with love. The man who would aspire to fatherhood in the clerical or lay state has to learn to love. He cannot be a browbeaten Dagwood or an absentee. He cannot be a patriarchal figure who tries to rule others by the force of his will. He can't treat people as though they were products in a supermarket. A father is not simply a foreman or manager. He has to be willing to take the risk of entering personal relationships — even with his disturbed or disobeying children. Too many so-called fathers, cleric and lay, disown their children as soon as they become troublesome.

The ancient Prophets tell us in the Old Testament that God accepted an imperfect people of Israel not as a hardened probation officer accepts another case on his load from a sense of duty or from a motive of higher pay. God is presented as the one who takes the initiative. And He is the One who initiates revelation of Himself. Without this self-communication in a visible, tangible way, there would have been no love relationship of Father and People. God made His Fatherhood more than a speculative thesis. He made His presence known.

By analogy with the history of Israel, every human father must make an effort at self-revelation if he expects love and recognition in return. Every day in our counseling we see examples of the distance between father and son or daughter. One boy complains: "I wish I could talk to my father. But he just won't listen. He can't understand why I can't get A's. All he can do is criticize." Another complains that his father considers him the "bad apple" of the family and will never listen or talk. The "communication gap" is not just a cliché for popularized articles on teenagers. A good segment of the adult world has tuned out on their children. They are afraid to reveal themselves by communication or any affective gesture.

There is no doubt that a similar communication gap exists between many priests and their people. I too must reveal myself before there can be any acceptance. Perhaps a first step to self-revelation is dissipation of any Sinai-like cloud surrounding the Sunday homily. What kind of a father speaks to his son with rhetoric and a textbook vocabulary? And what son appreciates being treated as a child with no judgment? I've heard sermons delivered to congregations of professional people which would insult the intelligence of an informed sixth grader. Just as some parents miss the radical intellectual and moral growth of their teenagers during the high school years, a priest may unconsciously treat his congregation as retarded infants. The high school senior who gets the opportunity of learning more theology than the college student of a few years ago will only scoff at a sermon which fails to recognize Vatican II. If a priest, for example, shows no consciousness of the laity's role, he will be judged fearful of losing his authority and will hardly be thought of in terms of a father. The dialogue sermon could help create a family atmosphere of give and take. How many of us are willing to take the risk of possible contradiction?

Revelation and acceptance! These are the keys to a spirituality of fatherhood. Just as God worked with an imperfect people, a father must accept people as they are. I may not like a teenager's attitude toward authority, or his long hair, but I must accept him. And if a man is to be a father, he must accept a person regardless of his background. King David had murder and adultery on his rap sheet — hardly a socially acceptable background. Yet God did not exclude him from sonship and made the covenant of friendship with him.

It's hardly ideal for the father of a family to show affection to one son and treat another as an outcast. Often Christianity gives the image of a similar exclusivism. There are the myriad sects with their peculiarities. And amid this sectarianism the Catholic priest may appear as a kind of scoutmaster of his own troop. If he doesn't identify with all men, "Father" is hardly a fitting title.

Exclusivism has many guises. I refuse the dinner invitation of a slightly neurotic and poor person because "I don't have time." But somehow I find time to accept the invitation of a potential benefactor or one who is charming and entertaining. A beggar comes to the door and I judge him a liar without hearing his story. A teenager gives me his opinion of the Church and I feign interest, but I have really tuned-out because he is a teenager. A group of young people ask for a folk mass and I put them off. I unconsciously say to many people: "I will be your father if you conform to my likes and dislikes, my values, my kind of Christian perfection."

Those of us involved in Catholic secondary education are aware of a subtle kind of exclusivism within the schools. The child from the lower class poor is automatically excluded. Many of our schools are limited to the upper middle class, white-skinned youngster. Should not the fatherhood of God urge us to waive certain projects (worthy in themselves) in favor of scholarships for the needy?

Besides the exclusion of the poor, Catholic secondary schools are often exclusivist towards the problem child within the school. Traditionally, the boy who is caught in a serious infraction of the rule (for example drinking in public) is expelled. He is usually rejected for the sake of the school's reputation and the protection of the other students. But who picks up the pieces when the potential alcoholic, drug addict or psychopath is expelled? He and his problem are usually shuffled on endlessly. A true father doesn't send his son to a boarding school when a behavioral problem arises. Likewise, it seems in accord with the ideals of Christian fatherhood that problems be worked out within the Catholic school structure. The Church need not fear a reputation of associating with outcasts and rejects. Christ was severely criticized for the company He kept. I heard a learned man once say that the only segment of Christianity really interested in the outcast was the Salvation Army. The greatest criticism one could aim at any father might be: "he is generally kind and loving to his well-adjusted children, but he rejects those with problems."

Today we are conscious of the numerous rejects and rejectors of society. There are the young who have lost all confidence in authority. There are the militant college students who defy the Establishment and reject the Church as its middle-class ally. Amid this general spirit of rebellion Catholicism symbolizes for many "non-acceptance." "Father" is often identified with middle-class values — "Johnny, you are my son, if you get a haircut every three weeks, get A's on your report card and don't get into any trouble." But if a man is really to become a father, he must accept those whose values he himself may not fully appreciate. His love cannot afford to be conditioned by social prejudices.

Jonah was greatly disillusioned with his success in converting the Ninevites. His pride was hurt when the dreaded enemies of Israel turned to "his" God. How could it be that a people who did not hold his values could be accepted by his God? But God proved to be more than a patron saint. As long as a man has Jonah's exclusivist hang-ups, he forfeits his title and gives weight to the fundamentalist's insistence that "no man be called father."

A theology of acceptance certainly pervades the documents of Vatican II. The renewed attitudes toward the lay and religious life, the stress on ecumenism and recognition of non-Christian religions, the willingness to admit mistakes, the concern for dialogue and cooperation with atheists all betray a spirit of fatherly concern and acceptance. If a spirituality of acceptance has yet to become widely identified with the hierarchical priesthood, the fault is not with the official guidelines of today's Church. It remains a strange paradox that there are men with ecclesiastical prestige who still only pay lip service to Vatican II, men who value positive law above the Spirit, judgment and retaliation above mercy, senile paternalism above fatherly acceptance. Unless a spirituality of fatherly acceptance based on the Gospel pervades all levels of Church life, widespread renewal is just another dream.

Chapter 7

Listening to All Voices

It's axiomatic to say that if the Church is to have a future, the young should have regard for its heritage, tradition and tried values. Yet today we witness a youthful distrust of the past and the values associated with the adult world. (I once saw a three year-old wearing a button: "Don't trust anyone over seven."). Tradition usually means nothing to the teenager who takes it for granted that he will someday visit another planet. He finds it hard to even think of anyone being over twenty. He considers anything that happened before the 60's to be ancient history. And like many in adult society, he is skeptical of structures.

I've talked to adults who are shocked and bewildered by the apparent iconoclasm of the young as they leave the institutional Church. Some of these adults, forgetful of their own youthful iconoclasm, adopt a hard attitude towards youth: "Let them leave the Church. Soon we will have a hard core of those dedicated youth, however few, who want to be part of the establishment." This reactionary mood of the adult world tends to measure virtue subjectively (sometimes just by age). And the criterion for following Christ seems to be steadfastness to not-thinking. Adults with this kind of myopia would canonize a system before a person.

Fortunately, the future of the Church depends on a free response to the Spirit of Christ rather than a pessimistic deduction from what appears to be logic. I believe there will be a future to the Church which will far surpass the Christianity of today's world. And if we adults are interested in this future we should listen to today's youth. We've heard the admonition to listen, but I don't think many of us really want to find out what the young are saying.

We too easily get threatened by the voices of dissent within the Church. But even amid the wild statements of "let's burn down everything," the young want some structure. And surprisingly they want to know the difference between right and wrong. But they don't want moralizing or dogmatic pronouncements. And many of us can't see the difference between a moral code and dogmatism. The young want to be told, not threatened.

If the young want to be told and not threatened, why do so many of them threaten the adult world? Why does the denouncer of structure himself become dogmatic and authoritarian? Why do we witness a new brand of infallibility in reverse which says: "All churchgoers are hypocrites." The old psychological mechanism expressed colloquially in terms of "like father like son" is definitely at work.

But if the young generation of Christians now assumes the role of pharisees, it is perhaps because the older generation has done too much preaching, answered too many questions, drawn too many lines between good and evil. And the young are unconscious imitators in their pronouncements.

Before preaching, an adult must listen. As a listener he will have to admit he doesn't have everything figured out. He will have to admit he has much to learn about God, people, life and himself. He must be sensitive to the voice of the Holy Spirit. Though it isn't easy for any older Catholic to think in terms of Pentecostalism, he must sit in silence with the young and listen to their prayers and aspirations. An adult must realize that the call of Christ is not heard in a complete sense, that perfection is not something one can possess like a new car. He must be convinced that the world is forever changing and can't rest content with the old comfortable cliché: "God is always the same."

I think the young have correctly detected that many adults fear listening. From political campaigns they've found out that people would like to rest secure in oratory about "apple pie and prayer" than confront realities of poverty. After all, if a politician uses the name of God he must be good. (Hitler and Stalin also used the name of God in their speeches). So I have to ask myself: "Do I really fear listening?" Some fear that if they listen to an agnostic, they too will begin to doubt. Or if they listen to a pagan they too will give up religion. This only shows personal insecurity. Listening is indispensable for growth. We can no longer afford the ghetto.

Christians have traditionally been poor listeners. Our conviction of truth has hardened our shell to voices from the wilderness. And despite our Master's injunction to "judge not," heresy-hunting has been one of our major sports. And because we have been convinced that Christ means fulfillment of revelation, we have viewed non-Christian religions with more condescension. Our attitude was hardened by our conviction that we possessed all truth. And when he spoke of "one, true, Catholic Church," the young have interpreted this as the arrogance of those who belong to an esoteric fraternity rather than to humanity.

I have a friend of 25, a man of high integrity who doesn't profess any particular religious faith. Yet because this young man is dedicated to the youth he teaches and coaches, I think of him as having encountered Christ. In accepting his own humanity, in being compassionate to his fellow man, I believe he has in a sense made a surrender of faith. I know this sounds like heresy because faith should include the intellectual assent to "Christ is the Son of God." I realize that Christianity is not a doctrineless humanism. But I somehow feel in the case of this person that institutionalized Christianity has made it nearly impossible for him to investigate Christ. And institutional religion has such a courtroom, inquisitorial atmosphere surrounding it that honest men look elsewhere for the humanism they desire. I believe this man would have no problem accepting the Christ who ate with public sinners. But he would have an almost impossible psychological obstacle to ask for Baptism. Yet I can say that in knowing this person and listening to him, I have discovered another dimension of Christ.

In the past it seemed less shocking if Christians were

non-listeners. Society was tribal. The Irish lived with the Irish, the Italians with their own. Priests had all they could handle in ministering to their own in-groups. But the world has changed in the past few years. And anyone who can't see the sin of clannishness in the Church of today is an enigma to me. When I read and hear of Catholics referring to "ours" versus "theirs" and maximizing the problems of ecumenism, I get sick. Enshrined in ghettoism, we stand worn and pale like the statues in an old cemetery.

There are still many Catholics who feel we have nothing to learn from non-Catholics so why listen? They see no need to investigate Hinduism. Why should they investigate any system which falls short of the truth? They smile at the ascetic wandering through the wilderness begging his bread and never focusing his eyes on a woman. They may think of Hindus as those who sit in the lotus position and contemplate the futility of human effort. They are satisfied with stereotypes and never realize that the Spirit speaks with many voices.

In the past we didn't listen to the pagan experience. We saw superstition in their deification of nature. And today many adult Catholics will not concede that the music or art of the young world has any revelation. Yet we deified Jansenism — the judgment that the human body was bad — and we still feel the effects of venerating this idol. The pagan could at least recognize some divinity in the ocean's roar or in a fertility dance. But we sometimes can't hear the Spirit in those around us.

Unconsciously many adults carry this exclusivist mentality even when trying to be ecumenical. And the young pick up this attitude. An adult should be more concerned about being an inquiring listener than one who possesses all truth. Christ didn't look for religious geniuses when he selected his disciples. He gave leadership to a man who found ideas difficult. But this man, Peter, was willing to listen and to learn by his mistakes. He was a man who had to eat his dogmatic pronouncement: "I don't know the man." He was a man who was willing to listen and be led into the unknown. If we regard Christ as "known" I think we have a problem.

Chapter 8

Can One Really Turn the Other Cheek?

In traveling from parish to parish I always find it disheartening that so few young men attend Mass or receive communion. As a high school religion teacher I've experienced more than a little anguish over the fact that boys give up their faith so easily during high school and college years. And so I ask myself again: "What are we doing wrong in our presentation of Christ? Do young men simply see Him as the 'bearded old lady' of poor art? Why doesn't he evoke the deepest stirrings of a man's desire to be a man?" I don't claim to have the theoretical answers. I know that a young man's faith needs the supportive example of priests whom they regard as men. And they need to reconcile the concept of manly strength with Christ's teaching on non-violent retribution. In this chapter I would like to explore this idea of non-violence and manliness in the context of a conversation I once had with a young man who converted from Catholicism to Islam.

Marv, age 30, was raised in a strict Catholic family

which he described as conservative. After attending a Catholic grade school and high school he joined an order of teaching brothers. But a year of the religious life was enough for him. He decided he wasn't qualified for a life in the classroom. He then joined an order of lay brothers and tried to live the life of the vows with as much perfection as was humanly possible. "Loss of his soul" seemed to be uppermost in his motivation, and after seven years as a religious he took the advice of a priest and left. Within a few months he married.

Though Marv left religious life, he still yearned for a life of ascetical perfection. He made a Cursillo and felt he had experienced Christianity at last. But as he reflected on his life experiences, he came to the conclusion that even the Cursillo enthusiasm could not answer his religious yearnings. Upon investigation of Islam, he decided that there was a basic problem with Christianity itself — or at least the Catholicism he experienced. Being one easily threatened and brow-beaten, he discovered a new source of energy and personal dignity in the teachings of the Koran. He learned that he "did not have to turn the other cheek." He found more or less the same moral code in Islam without the apparent self-annihilation imposed by Christianity. And the confusion he experienced in trying to pray to "three gods" was simplified.

As he sketched his religious history for me, I had no reason to doubt Marv's sincerity. He obviously had inner conflicts. The effect his new faith must have had on his devout Christian wife caused him anxiety. Yet he was determined to sacrifice his marriage for his belief.

After fifteen minutes of conversation, he asked me which corner of the room faced East. (It was sundown). Like a conscientious novice who fears the slightest deviation from the ascetical norms set by his master, he placed his prayer shawl on the conference room floor, faced what I called the "East" and recited his Arabic formula with the complicated rubrics of kneeling, bowing, standing. Though a Moslem can make exceptions to the rule of prayer at specific times, Marv was going to be exact. After the prayer, we continued our conversation.

My inclination was to say: "You've got to be kidding." My pseudo-analysis surmised that he was resentful of a failure to succeed as a religious. Or perhaps he needed an ascetical substitute which allowed for an unconscious revenge against a system which gave him guilt feelings. (I saved him my judgment).

When I suggested that he may have misinterpreted the "turn the other cheek" maxim of Christianity, Marv seemed threatened. I reminded him that Christ told his followers to be "wise as serpents" in maintaining their apostolic simplicity. And didn't St. Paul utilize his rights as a Roman citizen? Yet this did not contradict Christian submissiveness.

From this point our conversation took a turn towards apologetics. And I realized once again that nothing is accomplished by exchanging Scripture quotations. After arguing for a while, it seemed evident to me that Marv could not accept a religion which preached "someone else making atonement." His religious needs would only be satisfied by his own effort.

And if people ridiculed him for kneeling on his prayer shawl in public, he was willing to accept that kind of persecution. God was for him Someone who paradoxically did not need anyone yet who was somehow pleased by prayers said while faced in a certain direction and in a language hardly familiar to the worshipper.

Though it may sound paradoxical, I don't think Marv was ever a Christian. His "old faith" like his new faith in Islam had merely been a succession of practices, attempts to somehow placate a distant God. His old faith had never really been a commitment to a person but was rather based on extreme feelings of dependency and guilt. Marv was now coming of age, experiencing his human dignity. It seemed only natural to me that he would want to reject his neurotic, guilt-ridden religion. The only advice I could give him was to be honest about what he was rejecting. "Reject your past religion, if your conscience directs you," I told him. "But don't confuse your past religion with Christianity. Christian faith is commitment to a Person. It's that simple. If you have it, no new evidence whether it comes from heaven or earth will shake that faith. If you had been a Christian, no theoretical doubt about the possibility of a Blessed Trinity would have weakened your faith." (I gave myself an A for rhetoric).

Marv was visibly bothered by my attitude toward Jesus. He wondered why this "Son of Man" could not be accepted in the same category as Mohammed. He couldn't understand the fact that if one accepts Jesus at all, He is to be accepted in the terms in which He presented Himself. And Jesus plainly identified eternal life with Himself. One might say — as Marv tried — that Scripture is unreliable, or that the Councils distorted the true teaching of Jesus. But such accusations are purely gratuitous. Jesus cannot be put into our man-made categories. We either accept Him or reject Him on His terms and not in terms of how we would like Him to be. And I suspect that one who cannot relate to another person in any genuinely human way cannot accept the kind of relationship which Christianity is. This may have been at the heart of Marv's religious unrest.

Marv had been brought up with a Catholicism which looked upon doubt in terms of something morally evil. In talking to him it almost seemed that his new faith would never have been given a chance if there had not been the *Declaration on Religious Liberty* and the new spirit of tolerance within the Church. It almost seemed that he switched allegiances because he at last felt free to make a human decision. Repressed by a Christianity of fear, he could now stand on his own two feet. Previous religious superiors had warned him that it was "wrong to doubt" — even to doubt his vocation to the religious life. No advice could have been more harmful.

Some of the priests Marv consulted before seeing me dismissed him as a lunatic or one searching for an easier morality. I don't think his conversion was a rationalization to cover up a moral problem he couldn't face. The restrictions he placed upon himself under Islam rivaled those of a monastic order. He probably was sincerely looking for a serious religious commitment, found his experience of Christianity a source of humiliation and rejection and discovered a beauty which undeniably exists in the Islamic faith.

Marv's case may serve as a reminder that people are searching for dignity, discipline and brotherhood. Perhaps Christian love was present to some degree in Marv's everyday life, but it went unnoticed because it didn't have the emotional force of a Cursillo embrace or the precise structure of an Islamic rule. The fundamentalist is having an ever-increasingly hard time with the Christianity which is ever new and changing with the times. And perhaps this convert to Islam typifies in some way the religious person who cannot as yet encounter Christ, one who needs asceticism outlined in definite practices.

Vatican II would have us esteem the Moslem faith. I personally see Islam as analogous to Judaism — a tutor to the fullness of faith. Whether or not an individual conversion to Islam from a Jansenistic-tainted Christianity is the work of the Holy Spirit, I don't know. But cases like Marv's point to the fact that many people do need clear moral and ascetical guidelines and a conviction of their human dignity.

In retrospect I can better understand Marv's confusion with the Christian maxim to love one's enemy, the biblical injunction to walk an extra mile with the bad guy. I could personally better understand these seemingly masochistic injunctions in studying the life of Martin Luther King. Witnessing the charismatic power of this man even in death was a help to understanding the paradoxical nature of Christian non-violence. King's followers who put themselves on buses and in unwanted places were in the biblical sense turning the other cheek. Yet one could hardly call this timidity or passivity. The man being dragged from his sit-in position showed infinitely greater courage than the man with gun ablaze. As King so well recognized, passive resistance isn't really passive because man's spirit is using its unique force.

I must confess that I haven't seen too many Christians who live by the injunction to turn the other cheek. It's more natural to live by "an eye for an eye." Suffering and humiliation are not attractive. And it's no secret that they can easily turn to self pity. But the Christian who has once experienced the redemptive value in a refusal to seek revenge knows that non-violence is strength.

Chapter 9

The Catholic Pacifist

A boy approaching his eighteenth birthday confronted me with an uncomfortable question. "If you were eighteen today and didn't intend to be a priest, would you file for a conscientious objector's draft deferment?" I hesitated. When one is classified IV-D, his mind can easily avoid confrontation with such questions. Sensing my discomfort, the boy asked another question. "Can I really follow the teachings of Christ and run a bayonnet through a Viet Cong teenager?"

Though feeling somewhat unreal, I tried to put myself in the place of the young boy. I tried to wrestle with his problems of conscience on war. He was not a hippie, a coward or a member of a militarist group. He was just one of the growing number of young men who sought honest answers. I had to ask myself if there was such a thing as "Christian pacifism." Was it unreal for this boy to find the following of Christ and participation in warfare a contradiction in terms? It is easy to give a sermon on peace, to hand out glittering generalities. But how does one confront the practical question of conscientious objection? One can't honestly dismiss the CO with an oversimplification of "render to Caesar the things that are Caesar's." His position is more complicated than that of one who can't make the distinction between matters of man and God. Many in our society are conditioned to regard the CO as a coward. It is an easy stereotype which makes the user feel patriotic and brave. A Christian can't afford to fall victim to this kind of oversimplification.

Can there be such a thing as "Catholic pacifism?" It seems almost a tautology to ask the question. Christianity should mean peace. Perhaps another more specific question should be asked. Is one more or less a Christian when he refuses to fight in a particular war or any war in a combatant or non-combatant role? The question is hard to answer because the philosophy of pacifism has had many historical expressions. For some it is identified with ban-the-bomb demonstrations in London. Or the idea is associated with religious sectarianism. "Pacifist" for some means Quaker or Mennonite or "utopian." And because Catholics have for the most part served their countries in times of war, the concept of a Catholic pacifist seems contradictory. Thus it seems unusual when many young Catholic college students are registering as CO's. The facts show there are Christian CO's whether one argues pro or con for the reality of Christian pacifism. Tolstoy, Gandhi and Martin Luther King seem to reconcile non-violent resistance with the core of Christ's teaching and personality. And the young college student who is forming his conscience today is not seeking answers from moral theology texts on just or unjust warfare, but from the writings of Gandhi and King. These young men are reading, thinking and discussing the issue and are usually not ringing rectory doorbells for a clear-cut answer. Many are arriving by their own reflection to the conclusion that there not only is a Christian pacifism, but that the very meaning of Christianity is expressed in non-violence.

An honest CO is willing to take the Gospel literally when it says, "Love your enemies." He does not take lightly or try to explain away Christ's seemingly impossible command not to resist evil. He is willing to lay aside the norm of tribal justice, "an eye for an eye," and see what happens. He sees no justification for acts of violence in the name of patriotism. After watching an enemy executed via satellite or pictures of civilians maimed by bombings, he tells his countrymen that his loyalty will be shown by a refusal to serve. He does not judge the loyalty of the man who bears arms, and he asks that false motives not be imputed to him. The honest CO cannot take a flamethrower and burn out a group of the enemy hiding in a cave. He would rather die first. He finds it significant that Christ did not use force to overthrow his enemies on the eve of his arrest. If that historical fact means anything, the CO feels he has justification for not taking up arms. The violent man views Christ as a masochist or a fool. The CO who seriously follows the Sermon on the Mount finds in Christ the source of his moral strength. He may reflect on history and conclude that Christ's stance before Pilate was more powerful than any army. He may see in Christ's death a means for peace, more effective than any wars or treaties.

The young CO of today is usually not the doctrinaire pacifist of World War I or II. His thinking has been shaped by the bombs dropped on Hiroshima and Nagasaki, the prospect of a third world war with its aftermath of cave-man wars. He has seen war as it is on his TV screen and is not impressed by patriotic slogans. He seriously wonders about the waste of life in a war which is supposed to be saving people. He hears political analysts tell him that his death on a foreign battlefield is making the world unsafe for democracy, that American militarism is hindering rather than helping the cause of peace. He wonders why a fellow classmate who was noted for his violent aggression is praised as a loyal American when he enlists. He reads Pope John's *Pacem in Terris* and meditates on the words of Pope Paul to the UN — "War never again." He senses the impossibility of wars of liberation in a nuclear age. He senses with youthful vigor that no one wins wars.

The pacifism of many young men today might be summarized in the following creed.

"I believe in man as he is and can be. I don't believe in the utopian 'goodness' of man, that philosophy which says man will eventually solve his problem of hatred and wars. But neither do I believe in the total corruption of man or that wars are an inevitable necessity. I believe in what I see. And history tells me there have been few time-outs for peace. I can only conclude that mankind is either very stupid or has really never desired peace. I realize that I cannot erase stupidity or insincerity or hate by my personal decision. But I believe that my sincerity for peace is best expressed by my refusal to bear arms.

"I further believe that draft deferment should be based on something more real than theological hair-splitting on what one understands by "Supreme Being." And I think a person should be allowed to distinguish the difference between true self-defense and useless warfare.

"I don't believe nations should take out their inner frustrations by escalating warfare. To meet violence with violence is unchristian. War only generates more war. Peace is only generated by moral force."

Many of the new CO's are not the negative, individualistic pacifists who would logically have to answer "yes" to the question, "Would you allow a friend to be attacked while you stood by non-violently?" Theirs is not particularly the pacifism which makes one a doormat. Nor is it a creed of masochism. Believing in the Christ who said, "Be wise as serpents and guileless as doves," they attempt to bring together these opposites into an energetic, offensive yet non-violent resistance. They do not consider this weakness or submissiveness. They can reconcile their philosophy with the Christ who drove the sellers from the temple.

These new CO's find it difficult to answer the question, "Do you oppose all wars?" And they cannot say how they would have reacted to the draft at the time of Pearl Harbor. They merely reflect on the present. They find it difficult to make a clear distinction between "good guys" and "bad guys." The Vietnam War is not like a John Wayne western. While admitting that tyrants like Hitler had to be stopped, they wonder if presently a better method than war can be developed to prevent tyranny.

The young man's question still awaits an answer. "Would I be a CO if I were faced with the draft today?" I don't like to answer the question. It's too easy to give a yes or no answer when you are not personally affected. Yet as a priest, I cannot absolve myself from interest and involvement in the issue. I admire the patriotism and humanity of certain young soldiers. I admire the courage of certain young CO's.

This perplexing moral issue is given no black and white interpretation by the teaching authority of the Church. Yet Vatican II's document, "The Church Today," offers some guidelines. Positive support is expressed in this document for those who espouse non-violence. While not accepting or rejecting the arguments of traditional pacifism, it appeals for humane treatment of the conscientious objector. And because the document strongly condemns that type of warfare which involves civilian areas, it responds indirectly to the arguments of a CO who objects to a particular war because of mounting civilian casualties. Yet despite the increased clarity and sensitivity Vatican II gave to the questions of war and peace, the problem of the individual forming an honest conscience still remains. I can give a young man principles with which to form a judgment, but neither I nor anyone else can make that judgment for him.

As a child I was impressed by the adult world's

effort to teach me patriotism. Church and Country were two absolutes one didn't question. I was not brain-washed with a "my country right or wrong, my country" ideology, but the possibility of my country being wrong — especially in a war — was something unthinkable. Generals and Bishops were people we held in the highest esteem, symbols of the absolutes we didn't question.

After my training as a Jesuit which included seven years of philosophical and theological studies, I began to see loyalties in a different light. Study of the Church impressed me with the undeniable facts that churchmen weren't given the charism of having Christ's worldview. There was the Gospel of universal brotherhood and the historical facts of crusades and inquisitions. And so I began to develop a way of thinking which Christ called "being shrewd as serpents" towards those who by their office represented the authority. I developed a kind of reverential skepticism which questions severely the old maxim of the spiritual life: "The will of God is expressed in the command of your superior." The voice of an authority in the Church is not the voice of God when that authority has no faith.

I mention this fact of my personal psychology be-cause something similar is happening inside of young men. They can read history. They can see the repetition of human error taking place. They can see that the command to go to war does not reflect the will of God nor is it particularly a sign of true patriotism. And for this attitude they are considered cowards. Many of the boys I teach would not make any criticism of the military establishment or our nation's participation in warfare because they know they would be criticized by their parents. If a young man aligns himself with the pacifist movement, it is taken for granted by many adults that he appreciates nothing his country has done for him. To me it is the height of contradiction that a Catholic would not want to be known as a pacifist. (There are certainly idiot fringes connected with any movement, and of course the peace movement isn't exempt). Somehow we take it for granted that a Catholic can be spokesman for military virtues without embarrassment. But as soon as he aligns himself with the peace movement he is considered a communist.

I know a boy of 19 who left this country to avoid military service. He gave up everything dear to himself because of conscience — a conscience not respected by his draft board. There are bumper stickers which dogmatically assert: "America, love it or leave it." I believe this boy loved America and for that reason left it.

We don't live in the world of the 1920's or the 1940's. It's a world of peace or perish. And the Church should be at the head of the peace movement instead of reluctantly following for fear of being unpatriotic. I would like to see the day when Catholic and Christian are synonymous with pacifist.

Chapter 10

Catechetical Schizophrenia

Man's basic hang-up is his inability to match his actions with his words. He can sit on the veranda of an apartment building discussing ghetto conditions and not even take notice of the streets below him in flames. A social worker can give a layman the fine points of child psychology while his own children are being placed in the court's custody for neglect. This universal inability to put our resources where our mouth is may be a kind of "preacher's syndrome." The theologian would call it a result of original sin. The psychologist would call it schizophrenia. Whatever one labels it, it's real and hardly limited to the preacher man.

Anyone who would venture to teach the young must be aware of this basic schizophrenia of the human race. This is especially true for the catechist since proclamation of the Gospel demands a life style of charity to back up the theology of love. Oratory which is not bound up with a service of love is the catechist's most dangerous weapon. It was precisely Christ's greatness that He could back up His words with actions. And if the Church canonizes anyone, it isn't because he or she left posterity with a great collection of sermons.

Just what does preaching or catechizing mean today? How does one begin to communicate the Gospel? The very word "preaching" is not accepted by the young world. "Preacher" usually means "moralist" which in turn conjures up the image of one who sees no joy in living, one only interested in negative commands. The "Preacher" is the splendidly robed prelate uttering universal principles from some inaccessible pulpit or the party-loving parent who is always in a nasty mood towards her children. "Preaching" has become a kind of dirty word. And the style of today's catechist or parent who wishes to teach children about God must be disassociated from negative moralizing.

Anyone who wishes to communicate the Gospel should submit himself to a kind of self-examination which might include the following questions: (1) What do I really believe? (2) Do I express these beliefs in my preaching? (3) Do my beliefs represent the Gospel brought up-to-date? (4) Do my words correspond to my actions? (5) Am I adapting the message? (6) Is dialog integral to my faith? In short, what is the relationship of my words to my faith?

What do I really believe? Christ asked His apostles a direct question we all have to answer: "Who do you say I am?" (Mt. 16:16). He asks us this question again today. It's not: "Who does Theologian X or Y say that I am?" but "Who do YOU say that I am?" The German martyr, Dietrich Bonhoeffer, struggled with this question and became one of the most eloquent voices of our time. The circumstances of his life and the continual threat of death made him face the question just as John the Baptist faced it in Herod's prison. The Baptist preached Christ at the Jordan but really didn't grow up in the faith until pressed by circumstances and personal doubts. "Are you the one who is to come, or have we got to wait for someone else?" (Mt. 11:2).

Catechesis involves a struggle with personal faith which in turn involves a struggle with the mystery of suffering and the hiddenness of God. This faith must ripen into the realization that the God who is with us is the God who by all visible appearance has forsaken us. It involves a rejection of "Folk Christianity," the type of "religiosity" by which man calls on God only in distress. It involves the process of "coming of age" which John the Baptist and his modern counterpart, Bonhoeffer, experienced. Neither man was allowed to ascend a pulpit after their religious coming of age, but they closed the chasm between words and action. And their message is heard today because their actions correspond with their preaching. Whether or not one becomes a martyr, he has the same question to struggle with — "Who do you say that I am?"

The question directed to the apostles and us cannot be turned over to a theological faculty for an answer. It is not just a matter of speculative theology. The Christian catechist must personally face the "problem of Christ." A close friend of mine in the priesthood was bothered with this question and subsequently left the priesthood and the faith. Though it seemed on the surface that he left because of intellectual difficulties with the divinity of Christ, his motivation was not that simple. He was a man with great promise as a preacher, writer and catechist. He was not a recluse nor one embittered by the system. It seemed to me his basic difficulty was recognition of divinity in himself. There can be no foundation for the acceptance of the divinity of Christ if a man does not recognize the image of God in himself. It is not so much the complexity of the mystery of God which proves to be the stumbling block to faith. It is rather the complexity of the human personality, that schizoid condition St. Paul spoke of in terms of not doing the good one wanted to — that sense of guilt that results from feeling hypocritical — split. All these factors lead to disillusionment in oneself. And it is this basic disbelief in oneself that is the roadblock to belief in Christ.

Granted that I believe in myself, in others and in the mystery of Christ, I still have a further self-investigation to make before I get the "Good Preaching Seal." Is my orthodox belief translated into modern idiom? Have I absorbed Vatican II and am I able to translate the message to teenagers, dropouts, businessmen, college students and the ladies of the parish? There are men in the Church today whose personal piety cannot be disputed, but it is still the piety of their grandmothers. And a few things have happened since grandmother held me on her knee.

In speaking to college students and adult groups on the "Church in the Modern World," I am met with reactions which may be summarized as follows: "Do you really represent the Catholic Church or are you some kind of leftwing liberal? Do you mean that the Church allows for freedom of conscience and is really interested in the problems of men? I always thought of the Catholic Church as a kind of club, a group which was rather exclusive and not interested in atheists, Hindus, Moslems and Protestants." Twice in the past year I spoke in the classrooms of secular colleges and met this kind of unique astonishment at the proclamation of Vatican II's concern for mankind. The students had a stereotyped image of the priest as one who hands out moral maxims and clings to old mythologies. The astonished reactions I experience at the mere proclamation of Vatican II's insights leads me to a rather generalized conclusion that perhaps there is grave necessity for integration of its principles in my personal faith.

Besides integrating Vatican II, the catechist must learn to know and understand people. He can't shun active dialog. I might enjoy mystical communion with God yet be "from outer space" in the opinion of the young group I am addressing. I might be a fresh, creative thinker but have a mossback judgment, if there is not dialog with those I am trying to reach. How is my preaching to reach the college student who feels "emancipated from priestly witchcraft" if I don't speak to him in his categories? And how do I expect to reach a high school boy if I don't find out whether his problem is too much beer on weekends or the Mystery of the Trinity. One doesn't find the answers to the communication dilemma in Father Harding's *Homiletic Handbook* or Professor Crumm's *The Art of Preaching.* The principles are easy. The field work is difficult.

In searching for a style of catechesis we might take

inspiration from three men who did more than their share of field work in Christianity — Bonhoeffer, Martin Luther King and Pope John. We may not have had a prison-camp experience. We may not have suffered the humiliation of segregation. We may not be peasant boys turned popes. But the common denominator of the faith of these great Christian preachers is available to us — struggle. It is the same struggle St. Peter faced in the marketplace when he had to later prove his answer to Christ's question: "Who do you say I am?" It is the same struggle John the Baptist had to face — recognizing Christ in the depressing as well as the favorable situation. Effective communication is only born of struggle with faith, hope and love.

The problem of catechesis for most of us may be symbolized in the apostolate of the prison chaplain. He is a man who usually suffers from the impersonalism of the institution. He experiences disappointment because of conflict between the state's philosophy of correction and Christianity. He can do little to change the system that depersonalizes a man. He even feels that he has become a part of the system, that he will only be used as a part of the machine by the inmates. His tendency is just to go along with the impersonalism, to put in his time with the prisoners. But this means his death. His struggle is to show the most depressed of men that Christ is not part of any system, that He is the living God granting freedom to those who accept Him in faith. The institutional chaplain cannot influence others without his own struggle of faith, without resolving his own commitment and without dialog with the inmates. He can hardly pull out his seminary sermon notes for his homily.

The parish is not a prison. The pulpit is not a guard tower. The doors are not electrically controlled gates. Yet because of its size, the parish often succumbs to the failures of a penal institution. An answer to this problem of distance lies in the home Mass. Many priests have already found their own faith strengthened as well as that of their people by the atmosphere of dialog and friendship which surrounds the home Mass. Where the living-room couch has replaced the pulpit, genuine communication has often replaced "preaching." Closing the distance gap seems like an obvious first principle of catechesis, especially when it comes to dealing with the young. But it is the obvious we seem so reluctant to accept.

Chapter 11

The Gospel of Reassurance

The Catholic layman is generally surprised when he hears that the priesthood is not limited to men in black suits. The growing proclamation of this reality rooted in Scripture should lead to a new kind of Church where everyone feels a part and takes personal responsibility for the work of Christ. And while I try to spread a greater consciousness of this reality I need not fear a diminution of my priesthood of Sacred Orders. My priesthood and the layman's need never conflict in some kind of power struggle.

Many men in Sacred Orders today question the relevance of their state of life. Unconsciously they reason: "If the priesthood of the faithful is a share in the unique priesthood of Christ, what do I add by my witness." As a member of the hierarchical priesthood, I also undergo periods of intense self-analysis, wondering what precisely I am contributing to the Church. In this chapter I will let my thoughts run on in the second person — and hope that the reader will gain some further insight into the ministry of Christ's priesthood whether it is expressed by one in Orders or by one simply dedicated to the vocation of his Baptism. It is my conviction that all Christians are called to a ministry of reassurance, a ministry of building up the confidence of others.

You begin your self-analysis asking yourself if there is any meaning to your priesthood. You take inventory of your past month and wonder if you can list any accomplishments. You administered the sacraments. You preached. A few of the sick were visited and a grudging minimum of administrative work was done. You answered phone calls, made a few pre-marital investigations and wrote some letters. You spent time counseling teenagers and adults. You were busy. But did your ministry reflect Christ's? You didn't see the dead being raised nor the sick restored to a semblance of health.

You review your activities and wonder if priorities are given to the right people. You look at your desk and wonder what it looks like when cleared. There are those two paperbacks you intended to read, the unanswered letters and those enigmatic scraps of paper which you alone can decode. It's hard to imagine your life without phone messages.

You stare at the unanswered letters and promise yourself that you will answer — tomorrow. One is from a girl who is upset over her mother's drinking problem. She must have spent an hour carefully expressing her feelings that were up to this time guarded. She realizes you can't solve her mother's problem or restore peace to her home. She simply wants the assurance that someone understands her struggle. Your answer will mean something because you're a priest.

Another letter is from a nun who is discouraged

over the direction her community is taking. She feels that there is a kind of paranoid overreaction on the part of superiors to the new spirit of freedom. She tells you how her superior is issuing endless directives on points of discipline and warnings to those who won't conform. This nun who was beginning to experience a genuine freedom feels her community is regressing into an Old Testament spirituality where "law and order" reign supreme. And she doesn't want a Judge-God or a Cop-superior. Like the girl with the alcoholic mother, the nun realizes that there is nothing you can do about her superior. But she needs your reassurance that she has a grasp of Christ's law of love despite temporary setbacks in community life. She needs assurance that Christian life was not intended to be miserable.

Your third letter is from a man you baptized a few years ago. It is a manly expression of joy in a faith that hasn't grown dull. And for once you feel someone is giving you a lift. You're thankful for the grace he has received. You want to answer the letter with matching enthusiasm. But tonight you're tired and emotionless. Tomorrow.

To night you should answer the phone messages. Mrs. X. You know she will have several questions about the Pope's teaching on birth control. You save that one for last. Bill Y. He first contacted you through the suicide hot-line. So you waste no time in returning the call. It turns out that he hasn't slept for three days and his doctor (understandably) won't prescribe any pills. So you try to calm him down with a homemade recipe. Mrs. Z. You've been counseling her young son. You've neglected to see the boy for a couple of weeks. The boy has gotten into more trouble so it is time for you to see him again. Alice X. Long distance. You know she's a professional con-artist at 18. Her wrist has been cut so many times she can't type. She probably needs money or a home. Her county wants to get rid of her and would gladly release her from parole if you take responsibility. You call. You're right. But you don't have any plan for her.

You examine the notes of people who called. They don't bother you as much as the thought of several others with serious problems whom you've counseled. They haven't called because they don't want to "bother" you. You feel guilty in particular about two boys whom you know are dangerously experimenting with drugs. One of the boys is destroying himself and doesn't seem to mind. You know his mother. She is active in the church. She has no idea of her boy's problem. You wonder whether telling her in confidence will do more harm than good. You've got to call the boy and have another talk with him. He broke down a little the last time you made an effort. Perhaps now he is ready to get off his kick. Maybe he is just waiting for your reassurance. It all seems so infantile — this need to reassure people. But that's the way it is.

And just when it looks as though you will have time to catch up there comes the inevitable phone call.

"This is Joe. Remember me? I'm at the airport. I don't have any money. I need to talk to you."

You remember Joe all right. You worked with him a few years ago when he was a juvenile offender in another state. In a way you're glad to hear from him, but you are puzzled by his sudden appearance. On the way home from the airport he tells you of his plans to get a job and make something of himself. You look at his arms. They are still scarred with needle marks and you can't tell if any are recent. He assures you he hasn't been on drugs lately. There is one problem. He's jumping probation. Eventually, you realize, his probation department will have to be notified of his whereabouts. For the moment you find him lodging, and with the help of a friend arrange for a medical check-up and a job interview.

All the while you're doing things for Joe, you wonder about his motivation. Does he really want to start his life over, get off drugs and stop fooling around with the law? After a few days the truth seems to dawn. He's in the area because he's following a girl friend around who is trying to shake him. And you, priest and friend, are a "convenience" for room and board. You realize you're being used, but helping Joe is not a total waste of time. You are able to convince him to call his probation officer, go back to his home state and get the psychiatric help he needs. It seems like a little thing — giving a mixed-up adolescent a small degree of orientation. It's taken a good portion of your week. And you think of the others you didn't see.

In a sense, Joe is a symbol of your main apostolate. You didn't do much of anything for a boy who seemed to hit rock bottom. But he got a little reassurance from the person he used. Maybe someone else would never have made the first move of picking him up from the airport. Joe would have survived, and you would have saved all that time. But where do you draw lines? It's better to err in the direction of offering help.

You have a tightly scheduled weekend. Saturday night you receive a call from a friend who says there is a patient in a convalescent hospital who called for a priest. You change your plans to meet this emergency. It turns out to be no emergency. The senile lady who supposedly asked for you doesn't want to see you. So you reassure her that if she should ever want to talk, you're available. At times you wish someone would reassure you that there is meaning in the seemingly trivial.

At Mass you read the Gospel passage: "Do not be anxious for your life . . ." And you see a meaning related to your apostolate, your main work of simply reducing the anxiety level of people. At the group home where you spend your off hours, you find yourself reassuring the anxious adolescent. A 14-year-old girl tells you how she wished for her mother's death because she embarrassed her in front of her friends. You try to tell her that her mother is a sick person and not completely responsible for her actions. Another girl is worried because her mother has been missing for several days. You try to reassure the girl that her mother will be found and given some help. But you really don't know, and you're not so sure the girl herself will not take off. You begin to realize that problems are endless and you have very few solutions. You wonder if there's an essential distinction between being a priest and a security blanket. But you have to face the facts. It would be nice if everyone was peaceful and secure. If this were the case you would be out of a job.

So you look forward to the next weeks. You wonder how anyone can think a priest's life is dull or that celibacy is irrelevant. You wonder if the charism of prophecy that Paul asked the Corinthians to seek isn't still a good thing. "Speaking for God" is a way of expressing a ministry of reassurance. And today when so many people apparently cannot face the reality of their lives, there is need to seek this charism. It is not a charism as dramatic as working miracles or even speaking in tongues, but it is the one most needed for our day.

Chapter 12

The Relevance of Suffering

When I ask a teenager what relevance he finds in the Church, he will usually respond with a kind of democratic indifferentism: "It doesn't matter what you believe as long as you do what you think is right." Granted the fact that teenagers rejoice in being outlandishly liberal, there is some reason for the anti-authoritarian mood. The image of the Church as one, holy, Catholic and apostolic doesn't quite penetrate through the divisions, timidity and ennui of churchmen and churches. The unique relevance of the Church becomes obscured.

But even a teenager will admit that it is easy to list defects in the structural Church. He knows that faultfinding can become a kind of ritual, a twenty-four hour devotion. It's my experience that the honest Christian is searching for relevance beyond the inevitable flaws in structure. He wants answers from those of us who are supposed to make the Gospel message relevant to the Twentieth Century. And so I ask myself from my inside position: "Where is the unique relevance of the Church? Are you nothing more than a very fine humanitarian organization which raises a voice for peace, operates hospitals and schools and tries to feed the hungry? And how can we measure our effectiveness?"

It would be nice if we could answer the relevancy questions by hiring a good statistician. But I don't think too many of us are impressed by particular statistics on the number of conversions or good works. Atheists also gain converts and do good works. Christian relevance seems to need another kind of measuring rod. And I think that measurement of relevance is the intensity of the life of one who lives in Christ. Since that last statement sounds like a pious cliché, allow me to introduce a person who convinced me of the Church's relevance.

Marie is thirty-three years old, the mother of six children and the victim of bone cancer which allows her at most a few months of life. She is one of those mothers so taken up with her children that she didn't pay too much attention to her aches and pains. When she finally went to a doctor, it was too late to do anything. At this writing she is in a convalescent hospital unable to make the slightest move without the most intense pain. And every time I visit her she is a little closer to death. Cancer never conceals its ultimate intent. But despite the inexorable nature of cancer, Marie is not just a statistic or someone waiting to die. Despite the horrors of her crucifixion, she has a strength and beauty which has no human explanation. Even the stranger who meets her for the first time is impressed by the power of her spirit.

In Marie I found the answer to the relevance questions. Her presence did more for me than all the ascetical practices invented by the masters of the inner life.

Without getting involved in questions of abstract theology, I knew she gave me the strength to say, "Christ is God." This in itself seems contradictory because suffering in the young and innocent seems not only useless and absurd but positively cruel. Yet Marie explained things to me that I could never explain from the pulpit or in a catechetical class. She told me by her silent self-acceptance that the Church is something more than an imperfect structure, that it's rather the power of Christ which cancer itself cannot diminish.

Life brings us in daily contact with people of all ages and backgrounds who feel irrelevant because they do nothing remotely spectacular. You visit a teenage girl in a psychiatric ward. She is obsessed with the conviction that she and the world have no future. You get a suicide call from a college graduate with all the goods of this world and he repeats plaintively: "What am I going to do?" You daily see people whose despair is symptomatic of our era of technological magic. And despite the great effort of our society to eliminate pain, suffering seems to be an eradicable part of life. Even a good psychiatrist cannot anesthetize the painful guilt of a woman who has been unfaithful to her husband. And doctors seem rather helpless to comfort the cancer victim. Faced with the fact of inevitable pain and suffering, we should be spokesmen of a Christianity which is capable of turning suffering into a sign of the power of God. In a person like Marie suffering was not a trial to be endured with stoic resignation but a gift. We need people like her to remind us of the true nature of our vocation. Those founders of religious groups in the

Church had more than ordinary insight when they insisted that their priests and religious take time to visit the sick despite their important duties. For it is only in the presence of Christ suffering in his people that theology and the meaning of vocation can come alive. When I brought communion to Marie I gained a kind of insight into the meaning of "This is My body" which I could not get by study, preaching or prayer.

The sight of Marie did tempt me to think: "God, how can you do this if you are good?" And yet I always left her presence with more faith. Her presence was a contradiction of the medieval spiritual saying: "As often as I went out among men I returned less a man." Though having no formal education, she taught me something the courses in theology couldn't — redemptive love. And when she spoke to me of her reverence for priests because of their dedication, I felt a little embarrassed. For here was a woman without sacred orders who lived a kind of priesthood I could only hope to attain.

In the presence of intense affliction I find myself praying for a miracle. After all, didn't Christ cure the incurable and even raise the dead? And haven't the documented accounts of Lourdes shown that the miraculous isn't out of date? Why, I asked myself, couldn't Marie be cured. Wouldn't it be more in conformity with God's providence that she take care of her children? Isn't it a plain fact of sociology that children without a mother run a greater risk of becoming delinquent or developing emotional problems? Why her and not some woman who is selfish and spiteful, someone who never wanted children or contributed to the human love deposit? Why not an intervention if 'faith could move mountains'? I pondered these questions (perhaps naively) and began to realize that a miracle was taking place as her hands grew blacker and the fullness of her face receded into skeletal outlines. I began to realize that something supernatural was taking place as she more and more became the sacrament of Christ's presence.

Today we are emphasizing the Church's mission to feed the hungry and shelter the homeless. Some missionaries are even spending more time and effort in teaching agricultural methods than in catechizing. We recognize the importance of alleviating human misery before Christ can even be preached. Yet with this renewed emphasis on alleviating misery, we can't afford to forget that suffering will be present to the human condition despite affluence. Thus while pursuing a just social order we must penetrate more deeply into the mystery of suffering which human effort can alleviate but not ultimately eradicate. I think it is precisely here in the presence of human misery that the Church as the extension of Christ is relevant — not as an opiate but as a conscious source of strength. The Church has a gospel of resurrection with Christ through suffering with Him — a gospel some of us seem to have forgotten.

If we are to preach Christ to modern man I think we will have to further explore the mystery of suffering. And I think our best guide is a person like Marie. As I witnessed her crucifixion I became puzzled by the fact that there were still divisions among Christians. How absurd a family argument appears in the face of a dying person. As Marie expressed a desire to be reconciled with a woman who wished her harm, it became clear that the perpetuation of division is a symptom of psychological childhood. And it seemed to me that much of our piety revolving around the Crucifixion of Christ is still infected with a kind of medieval sentimentalism. We shed tears for a past event but will not bandage present wounds. When we finally decide to understand the meaning of Christ's suffering we will forget the theoretical arguments which divide us.

Modern man's reluctance to explore the depths of suffering is not only manifested by the doctor who will not tell a patient he is to die. There are signs of this mentality in our catechesis. Perhaps in reaction to the macabre way death was popularly presented in missions and retreats we shy away from the topic. Yet I would think an awareness of suffering — not simply theoretical — should permeate our faith.

Chapter 13

Neither Liberal Nor Conservative

The author of the letter quoted in this chapter is a 21-year-old college student. Raised a devout Presbyterian, she came to Catholicism a few years ago to fulfill her personal religious aspirations. She has always regarded her new faith as fulfillment rather than conversion. And today she struggles with many of the problems and doubts of the proverbial "born Catholic." She asks the same question St. Paul asked the Corinthians: "Is Christ divided?"

Though personal letters usually have a very limited value, I think this letter may be of interest. This girl's thinking reflects the sentiments of many Catholics both young and old. She speaks for many of today's fervent and intelligent believers who refuse to be labeled liberal or conservative or subscribe to factions.

"Father, I'm sure you're aware of Masses being said by priests who have married and by priests who who are suspended. You know of the inter-faith services, the fact that in some places Protestants are encouraged to receive Communion. You know of experimental liturgies, those blessed and those unblessed by authority. Some of these phenomena are confusing to me.

I know that you love the Church, and so I ask you the following questions in all sincerity. Do you find the rubrics of the Mass and the regulations for Confession unsatisfactory and outdated? Do you consider the Pope's encyclical on birth control binding on the conscience of the Church at large? Is authority in the Church under the guidance of the Holy Spirit and to be obeyed as such; or is hierarchical authority irrelevant in a democratic society and should we rather listen to the voice of the Holy Spirit in our own individual situation? Should we support the 'underground Church' and interfaith communion? Is a more conservative attitude worthy of censure as 'cowardly and unthinking?'

"All this outburst of confusion is the result of pressures I feel from so many sources to declare myself a 'leaping liberal' though I question the validity of much enlightened thought. Of course, I don't have to 'declare myself' anything. But I find myself so confused. I wonder about my spirituality. Is it too conservative, 'built on sand?' Do I wrongly desire the kind of security one can't have in our shaky world? If I do not go along with more liberal thinking, am I blocking the action of the Holy Spirit in my life? I realize how unfair it is to ask you to generalize about such sensitive questions. The Church is being split; the rift is widening daily. And all this seems a betrayal of Christ who prayed for our unity.

"The Mass has been very precious to me, its prayers largely satisfying. The dogmas of the Holy Trinity and the Virgin Birth do not throw me for a loop. Furthermore, celibacy in the priesthood means to me that I have a special claim upon every Father, that each is my brother in Christ, and that I can love each with a genuine love which I have never considered immature.

"I guess I've had very fortunate experiences in confession, for I seldom leave the box without feeling that Christ has spoken in the counsel I've received and that I have a clean slate and a new challenge to work with.

"There are times I wish the Eucharist could be celebrated in the intimacy of a home. I long for a more carefully considered homily. I wonder if perhaps my conservative upbringing has made me less a part of my own generation than of the one gone by. Perhaps I am unusual and should 'get with it.' But why should I pretend? I find singing on the way to Communion distracting at times. And I honestly appreciate kneeling at Communion to the other 'assembly line' technique. Some say we should receive Communion in our hands. I don't see how this would be more liturgical or personal. That's the way they give out Communion in the non-liturgically orientated churches.

"The birth control encyclical was unsettling primarily because of the general 'don't-pay-any-attention' attitude which followed its publication. I feel sorry for the position you priests are in when guilt-ridden couples come to you for advice. The public seems to feel that disagreement with the encyclical disregards the Pope's authority. There's the misconception that every papal statement is a matter of infallibility and that reaction to this statement is a denial of the Pope's authority.

The secular press has made any kind of objectivity almost impossible with its shouts of "Pope Forbids Use of Pill" or "Pope Bans All Birth Control." It could be that the Holy Spirit was trying to say something through Paul in an age of apparent absurdity.

"Father, I do not consider myself a 'conservative' in the sense that word is used in the Church — one who closes his eyes to the work of Vatican II. I live with Lutherans and feel a deep sense of unity with these girls. We experience our Christian commitment and discuss theology without partisanship. I am so happy in my faith, I envy myself. Yet I wonder if I am too complacent and too much to the right. I hope there is room in the Universal Church for those with a more radical bent and room in my heart to listen to them and love them."

I could hardly read such a letter without asking myself: "What is the Holy Spirit trying to say to the Church?" And I have to agree with certain things the girl wrote. First of all, there has to be room in the Universal Church for various points of view. Should a bishop suspend a priest who contradicts him on a controversial issue, it usually manifests a threatened authority rather than a threatened Church. People are more disturbed by such an action which implies that the Church only accepts a party line, than they are by a priest's imprudent utterances. A Universal Church has to be a Church of dialogue, not a Church of suspension and excommunication.

I personally don't like the idea of an "underground Church," i.e., grouping together to do those things that a particular bishop doesn't allow. Such movements often attract those with a superficial spirituality, people whose motivation is more "against" (Bishop X) than "for" (Christ). Yet I can understand why people join the underground. There is a clerical mentality which seeks to perpetuate a mechanical spirituality, which fears liturgical adaptation as though God is disturbed by certain formulae and placated by others. I think that a priest should have more freedom in adapting the liturgy to the needs and mentality of his congregation. But this implies that when one is ordained he has a well developed sense of the sacred and won't turn Mass into a circus. There is obviously not that kind of trust put in the men ordained. The existence of an underground Church clashing with the institutional structure shouldn't have to be in a Church which is truly universal.

I agree with this student's view that there was an over-reaction to the Pope's encyclical both on the part of "liberals" and "conservatives." There were priests who preached "vengeance" sermons on the encyclical, men who went beyond what the Pope wrote. They assigned degrees of guilt, reviewed the list of possible contraceptive practices and threw around the term "mortal sin" as though they were the final arbiters of conscience. The tone of their sermons reflected their personal disgust with the opinions of learned theologians and gloated with an "I told you the liberal priests were wrong all along" attitude. Such priests are more interested in an abstract principle than they are in human feelings and in the complexity of the birth control issue as it exists in a real context. On the other hand, there were those who denounced the encyclical simply because it was traditional. Perhaps they could have asked themselves if there was not the very truth in the Pope's thought which is needed in our atmosphere of moral relativism.

If this student's letter reiterated any central truth, it is the practical truth of the first Pentecost — that the Holy Spirit doesn't cause narrow partisanship, that one doesn't have to allign himself with a "camp" and declare himself conservative or liberal, a supporter of the underground or the *status quo*. St. Paul seemed capable of resolving conflicting tensions in his expression of Christianity. We should be capable of doing the same.

Chapter 14

Thoughts At the End of A Day

One of the girls I counsel told me that each evening before falling asleep she reviews every action and attitude of her day. I thought this kind of introspection rather amazing for a fifteen year old. My early guides in religious life made an attempt to instill in me a habit of reflective self-examination. But it was at a time when my day consisted of memorizing Latin and washing floors. Reflection then seemed a waste. In those days I kept a diary of my inner life — long since discarded for lack of content. Now, at my present stage of life, I find every day filled with people and events worth a meditative reflection. So taking a cue from my teenage friend, I'll let my thoughts this evening run loose for a while. And though I don't claim to be a Malcom Boyd or a Michael Quoist, I'll let these reflections slip into the literary form of a prayer.

"Lord, how do you counsel a boy when he isn't sure he is alive? The conversation I had with Phil today didn't seem real. I think he was still in a state of shock from the accident he had last weekend. (Tell me, how does a person end up at the bottom of a river with his car?) I think the greatest proof of providence is the fact Phil is alive. (I know he's still waiting for the wreckers to find his car, so he can rest assured his body is not in it.) It seems that an encounter with near-death is the only thing that can impress some teenagers. It seems that my role as a priest is simply to be available to interpret the meaning of You when something happens to boys like Phil.

"Lord, sometimes I wonder about our Catholic educational system — especially after days like today. Every time we discuss capital punishment in class I wonder if we have progressed beyond those tribal societies which demand an "eye for an eye." Take Karl, for example, I'm sure the kid has never gotten in trouble in his four years in high school. I would say that he is a symbol of private virtue. By the way he expressed himself in class today, I would guess that his solution for the rapist-killer would be to have some kind of public molester and hatchetman give the depraved sex killer an exact measure of retribution. I wonder why so many kids can't see an issue like capital punishment in a wider social context — not to mention a specifically Christian one. Perhaps they simply reflect the privatist ethic of their parents. (But I don't want to get on that subject.)

"Mike gave me some of his poetry to read today. You know, poetry — even the poorest — is great when you know the person trying to express himself. Most of the boys make fun of Mike because of his appearance. Yet he is way ahead of them. He has a sense of the mystery of life. It seems he almost needs poetry as a kind of prayer, a kind of justification for his living.

"Lord, what do you tell a sixteen year old who won't budge on the point of Mass. He sees no value in going. He's not an irreverent boy, and he doesn't lack intelligence. I've done my home work on him. He's not insensitive. His parents are sincere Catholics. It's not a matter of his having no example. He isn't lazy. He's always doing personal favors for me. He doesn't really have a hangup with sermons, priests and poorly conducted liturgies. It's hard to pinpoint his problem. I think he wants attention. Well, that's not such a bad thing, but how do I get him to see Mass as something good? He sees it as a source of conflict in his family, something which drives him further away from his parents. He admits that even with the liturgy conducted perfectly, he wouldn't attend. Who has failed? I'm his religion teacher. He comes to me for advice. And I can't give him a convincing motive for loving the Mass. And I know he's not the only one. Lord, I know the answers lie deeper than liturgical reforms. I know this boy is searching for a relationship. He really isn't looking for my logical arguments on "why one should go to Mass." He's testing whether I'll accept him for what he is. Am I wrong for not worrying about his present skepticism?

"Why do we fail to see ourselves with the clear perspective of the young? Why do we turn to rationalizations when there are scandalous contradictions in the Church? A student asked me how the Church can put missing Sunday Mass in the category of mortal sin — like rape. And another asked why I'm permitted to say a home Mass while a priest in another diocese is suspended for the same deed. And I must confess, Lord, I don't know all the 'why's.' Why is Sunday Mass under the obligation of mortal sin? Who is really motivated by the threat of sin? Most teenagers are challenged by threats to do the opposite. And is that person who attends Mass simply to avoid "contracting a mortal sin" really performing a religious act? I thought freedom was the essence of our act of faith. Or have I misunderstood Your Gospel? So what could I tell my student? Yes, I know the difference between the objective act and subjective dispositions. I know there has to be full consent of the will. But what if this boy's father missed Sunday Mass from sheer ornery, fully-consented laziness. Those who emphasize willfull missing Mass to be a mortal sin sometimes give the impression that liturgical laziness is as serious as murder or rape. After all, a mortal sin is a mortal sin. Lord, my student was confused. He thought I was avoiding the issue with my circumlocutions to avoid the terminology of mortal sin. Isn't it time we changed some of our expressions? Isn't it time we broke from our Kantian mentality of "duty," "obligation," and "you better love God or else He'll get you?" It's true that many people only get serious when threatened. But don't we promote an infantile attitude toward faith rather than encourage adult response? Do we fear people will no longer flock to our churches if we drop the big sanction? Is there something wrong with us?

"Lord, I'm running into more Catholics who have a distaste or an absolute block for private confession. I guess I've grown used to the convenience of religious life. This evening I went to a friend's room and confessed in the context of a friendly conversation. There are a lot of people who would like to be able to speak familiarly with a priest. But there is no opportunity. The people I've talked to lately tell me they don't want to be simply a voice any more, getting three hail Mary's from another anonymous voice. They don't want the feeling that they are being hustled along for the next in line. So what's the solution? General absolutions? These people still have the desire to have a personal confessor. I still can't believe what I heard a pastor tell his congregation last Sunday: "You people are arrogant in asking for a confessor out of the appointed Saturday hours." So it's obvious that there are problems at both ends. Help us to find solutions. These complaints about the impersonalism of confession don't come simply from the iconoclasts. They come from those followers of Yours who have never committed any serious sins. They are now beginning to question that "grace" which comes automatically from a sacrament. They don't understand how an experience which is so frustrating can be a vehicle of Your love. I believe in the power of Your sacramental presence. Why are we afraid of reshaping the Sacrament of Penance? Why don't we have short penitential services before Mass and give general absolution to the faithful? Is our mentality that shown in the story of Jacob and Esau? Do we fear unworthy people will "steal absolutions?"

"You must have a special place in heaven for those who work with grade school kids. I thought high school boys were difficult to teach. That CCD Mass for those "Inner-city fourth graders" this afternoon was an experience I won't forget for a while. I'm glad I walked over to those girls who were huddled in the corner before Mass. Unlike high school kids, they didn't try to disguise their conversation. They spoke very candidly about how they were going to "beat up Maria after Mass." (It seems that Maria had hurled insulting epithets at one, Nia.) Well, Lord, it may have been unnecessary to have omitted the gospel for the day. But at that time it seemed more fitting to paraphrase the story of the woman caught in adultery. I made a big point of the fact that people wanted to settle a point by throwing rocks and that You said this was no way to do it. The kids listened intently. They knew the application of the gospel. They all went to communion, and for a moment I felt they had scrapped their plan to "get" Maria after Mass. Well, they were still intent on a fight after the "go in peace." But I think they got something from the liturgy. I guess the law of revenge is learned early in life and is only unlearned through some pretty hard effort. No wonder you had such harsh words for those who scandalized the young."

"Lord, don't forget Mrs. Y. You gave her several children. And by some inexorable law of disease her cancer only gives her a few months of life. Help her to accept what none of us understands. How trivial every human problem seems in comparison to that of orphaned children."

Chapter 15

The Moral Values of Today's Youth

Morality is difficult to define. It is popular to describe it simply in terms of the cultural mores of an individual or group and assign no intrinsic rightness or wrongness to human actions. Some think of morality exclusively in terms of sexual behavior. For them, the immoral person is the prostitute or adulterer, etc. Others of a more cynical disposition will describe morality as a "man who wears a black suit with a turned-around white collar."

In trying to define the morality of today's youth, I recalled two recent experiences from my avocation of picking up teenage hitchhikers. Hitchhiker "A" was a crew-cut, straight-looking college student of about 19. His sports car broke down, and he needed a 20 mile lift into the nearest town. The day was hot, and I inconvenienced the overly-crowded group of boys with me by stopping several times to seek help for "A". Not once during the ride did he show any sign of appreciation, nor did he say "thank you" at the end.

Hitchhikers "B" and "C" were a seedy-looking,

long-haired, boy-girl pair — also about 19 years of age. Only as I pulled over to pick them up, did I notice they had two dogs with them. They got in and made no attempt to control their pets who seemed to enjoy licking my ear and chewing on a seat belt. The hippie twosome seemed surprised at my annoyance with the overfriendliness of their dogs. But they did at least manage to say "thanks" at the end of the ride.

I cite these examples as a prelude to understanding youthful moral values, because I believe morality has to do with all human behavior — the controlling of one's pets as well as controlling one's sexual drive or urge to kill. I believe morality has to do with a person's ability to express gratitude for small favors as well as for the gift of life.

It's easy to criticize the behavior of young people. So for the moment I'll aim at adults who try to pass themselves as the exemplars or spokesmen of morality. In particular I would like to complain about those who show grave concern about the problems of violence and sex in movies, obscene drama on the college campuses, pornography in the newspapers and the kind of sex-education given in the schools, but have little sensitivity towards the issues of race relations and war. This "moral sense" doesn't want to discuss the boy who is shipped back in a box from Vietnam but shows horror over nudity in films. While not denying that the question of "how much of the human anatomy may be exposed in public" deserves some attention, this moral stance seems obsessed with it.

This adult mentality I speak of sees many enemies of morality in the United States. These enemies are humanists, social scientists, evolutionists and historians who debunk much that was held sacred in our traditions. And last but not least of their enemies is sex-education in the schools. This mentality seems to think that moral decay is something new in the U.S. When I read about our society of a hundred years ago I can only conclude we have made some moral progress. There is much more concern over feeding the poor and housing the homeless. I can't subscribe to the mentality which yearns for the days of our Founding Fathers and their concept of religion and morality. There has been an evolution. A good person of today couldn't justify a household slave. That old time religion which justified segregation was a bad religion no matter how many scriptural quotes were used to explain its position. American Tradition can be worshipped as a false god. And if I say many youth are today more moral than our renowned ancestors, it is not simply to their credit. Morality is an evolving social reality to which our generation made its contribution.

The traditionalist, static, individualistic, natural law outlook on morality is pious, but it really stops short of a mature Christian ethic. There are greater problems than obscene drama on college campuses. There is a stage of moral development which goes beyond fear of one's enemies, a morality which concentrates on the promotion of the sanctity of human life. And I believe many youth profess such a code despite their apparent indifference to a fundamentalist interpretation of the Decalogue which fails to apply "Thou shalt not kill" to warfare.

But "Youth" as well as "American Tradition" or "Natural Law" can be made a false god. And much of the praise given the younger generation is nonsense. Youth has its share of moral primitives, those whose ethical norm is "how far can I go before getting caught." Many adults in business, medicine, government and the Church have taught them this norm so characteristic of children who only understand the motivation of fear of punishment. A classic example of this primitive moral level was evidenced in the interrogations of those teenagers who in 1957 stabbed to death a 15 year-old polio victim in a New York park. The remorse felt by the young murderers was limited to sorrow for getting caught. This mentality with its various degrees of intensity is not absent in the young world. Some regress to this kind of a "moral norm" only temporarily. For others it is a life style. It's common to find a youngster who will only feel this kind of negative remorse when caught cheating or shoplifting. "I wasn't hurting nobody," they will rationalize. Many of these itchy-fingered ones will respond to an adult taking interest in them. They show capability of moral development if personalism enters their lives. I think many young people at this primitive stage of a "how far can I go" ethic show more hope of moral progress than those adults entrenched in their self-righteous, individualistic, law-and-order morality. I can easily understand a 16 year-old girl who shoplifts a new dress to keep up with her schoolmates. But I find it difficult to understand a bishop who uses police force to keep his priests in line. I really don't think those good but trigger-happy individuals who constantly speak of law and order have advanced beyond the dead legalism Jesus condemned for giving man-made regulations priority over man. Those entrenched in the law-and-order moral mentality experience legal purity when someone is arrested but really don't worry about basic rights for everyone.

Many upper-middle class youngsters have this law-and-order moral stance. They dress neatly, wear conventional hair styles, abide by most of the school rules and those of society — except for occasional drunkenness and property smashing. They generally have the virtues outlined in the Scout Handbook. But many of them have blind spots when it comes to questions of racial justice or the plight of a minority group. They find it hard to understand anyone outside of their social milieu. Years of "religious education" do not erase the use of "nigger" or stereotypes such as: "why can't they make it on their own like we do?" They resent it when a minority teenager is given a job priority. They call all draft resisters "cowards." They do not challenge institutions with any seriousness — whether it be a static parish church or capital punishment. In college they may become political activists but it just turns out to be sentimentality without any deep roots. And after college they will generally settle down to middle class obscurity and share their neighborhood's fear of "Negroes moving in." Their moral evolution gets beyond the jungle but stops short of Christianity.

However, there are youth today whose moral development reaches the kind of personalism described by Paul in *I Corinthians*. They really do delight in truth and are ready to endure, trust and hope. They do get beyond the talking stage when it comes to the great issues of our time. They are concerned enough about the wages given to a grapepicker to submit themselves to the ridicule of a picket line. They do give their spare time to tutoring the young. Their love for America and the Church goes beyond flagwaving and clichés. Many of these youth are willing to sacrifice themselves for their fellow man.

I believe we have today an atmosphere in the Church and in society which allows youth to reach a high moral level. I think it is a healthy thing that my students can challenge everything I put forth as true. I think it is healthy that a young person can question the validity of certain kinds of ecclesiastical and secular power, that they can question the validity of participation in a particular war or the police practices of a certain area.

Youth will be as good or as bad as we want them to be. If we repress their honest questioning they will leave the Church. I have little patience with those authoritarian parents and priests who rejoice in rejecting rather than in the truth. And when we reject the young, I think we have lost the battle for morality in society. If we are content with a philosophical analysis of youth's morality, we fit the image of St. Paul's tinkling bell.

Adults are today frightened by the phrase "new

morality." It brings up images of fornication, veneral disease and unwed mothers. The phrase seems to be the motto for those who wish to destroy the Church. People tend to associate "new morality" with the so-called sexual revolution which advocates the creation of "sex playpens" for children and adults. There is nothing really new about promiscuity and hedonism. Our civilization couldn't hold a candle to ancient Greece in this respect.

"New Morality" can mean something quite different than the relaxation of all moral precepts. It can mean the revitalized thrust towards personalization in our institutions and relationships. And this is the kind of new morality adopted by many of today's youth. The pot-smoking hippie is not really the spokesman for this renewal though he may be a symbol of the disillusionment with old structures. Nor is it the unscrubbed intellectual still struggling with his Oedipus conflict who is the spokesman for youth. There is a problem of leadership in the young world. And we adults often just sit in fear as though teenagers were unknowns from another planet. Or we feel that we have to wear beards and beads and utter "groovey" at least once a sentence. The teenager needs leadership. And the adult who is willing to break down the artificial distinctions between the generations and see all people as persons is in a position to lead youth in their quest for an authentic morality.

Chapter 16

Ministry on the Edge of Hell

It's 2:30 am. You're driving to meet a total stranger whose last words to you were "you don't really want to help me." You arrive at the address. The door is open. You hesitatingly walk in and find two hundred and fifty pounds of hysterical manhood surrounded by cigarette butts and empty beer cans.

You discover that Burt is divorced, the custodian of four children and obsessed with loneliness and despair. Tonight he is thinking of suicide in the wake of remorse and fear over a homosexual act. He tells you how he boasted all his life about his non-belief in God. "God, who is She?" was the standard way he answered anyone who questioned his belief. Tonight he is crying out for God, for anyone who can tell him he is all right. He is disturbed by his bisexuality, his ugliness and his feelings of guilt. And though he is protesting against his feelings by a drinking vigil, he is quick to maintain that he has no problem with alcohol.

Burt is unique, yet his story runs like a familiar song. Loneliness, despair and awareness of a spiritual vacuum are recurrent themes with those who call you with the ultimate threat. They defy you to take interest in them. These are the inhabitants of their own despair, the almost lost ones who can't believe in their own worth.

Without drawing too close a parallel to police science, the Christian ministry may be expressed in terms of walking several beats. One of these beats (not a geographical area) I like to call the Edge of Hell. Those on the Edge have almost made a philosophy of Dante's admonition: "Abandon all hope those of you who enter here." But they don't quite enter that hell of non-communication. They can still reach for a phone.

There are no age requirements for the Edge of Hell, nor does this psychological area set any requirements for race, religion or sex. Humiliata lives there, and she is only fifteen. "I want to die," she tells you — hoping you will give assurance she has reason to live. Her story too is a familiar one. She knows nothing of her mother except for the fact that "she took off when I was a little kid." She has no memory of her father and only knows of his reputation for being "no good." The relative with whom she lives is an alcoholic. Her intense memories of childhood center around a preoccupation of having been sexually molested by older men. Now at fifteen she has entered into a sexual partnership with a man twice her age, previously married and without the slightest evidence of sincerity. And so Humiliata is tortured with an awareness of being used and caught up in the fantasy word of "happiness-ever-after." She is aware that this relationship will only bring emptiness, and yet she has no other formula for happiness. The embrace of someone using her for his own selfish pleasure seems to her better than total emptiness. And so realizing that she has nothing but a crippled ego, you gently but firmly try to give her direction. You realize she could use some professional help. And you realize that most on the Edge either can't afford or aren't disposed for psychiatric help. They simply cling to whomever can prevent them from going over the brink. Humiliata once swallowed a bottle of pills in a time of crisis, so she no longer trusts her own feelings. And she struggles in that savage world of fantasy hoping for happiness while feeling it is really beyond any real possibility. She is starved for love and security and grabs at anything — including the sexual act separated from love — to find happiness.

On the Edge of Hell there is also no segregation based on wealth. One would guess that Ron, age 60, had made it by the standards of success canonized by our society. He had two new cars, a sixty thousand dollar home with a swimming pool, a faithful wife and several children. He was a man of status and prestige and yet his emotional life was still in its infancy. He, like Burt, is a total stranger to you as you ring his doorbell in answer to a plea for help. Ron's home is impeccably clean without any remnants of a drinking vigil — except his breath. And so you listen as he too cries and repeats the question: "What am I going to do?" So you discuss motives for living — realizing all the while that you are not dealing with a classroom situation. Ron was college-educated and well-versed in the mechanics of logic and ethics. But he couldn't solve his own problem of despondence. At one point in our conversation he announced he was going to the bathroom to cut his wrists. And while I ordinarily don't follow people into their bathroom, I went along with his game simply to reassure him that he should stay alive. Obsessed with some kind of a demoniac force, he kept repeating the question: "What am I going to do?" And all I could think of was his material security and his years of education. There is sometimes no new answer you can give to those on the Edge. They simply need someone to cling to. Those walking this beat realize that a male must also at times play the assuring role usually associated with motherhood. I know that many men will not assume this role of reassuring the emotionally insecure. But I believe it is a sometimes necessary part of the Christian apostolate.

Some people seem to be permanent residents of the Edge of Hell while others move in and out. Not all are suicidal, but they are all at a loss to handle their life situation. Many of them can give good advice to others but cannot begin to solve their own problems. There are the parents who cannot begin to control or understand their teenagers. (With these one can sympathize.) They are the divorced women struggling to raise their children by holding down two jobs. Some of these women have been physically or psychologically beaten by husbands in quest of masculinity. And it is almost easier to restore a sense of dignity to the one physically beaten than to the one torn down psychologically. On the Edge are the young men who father a child but are unable to *be* fathers, and who in some cases stand by silently while the child is aborted. There are the nice-looking, well-dressed, silent teenagers who are within full of rebellion and turmoil.

In these communities which have restored the concept of the "cop on the beat," policemen have gotten to know the afmiliar faces in their geographical area. On the Edge of Hell there are always new faces, but the problems are much the same. And the priest on the beat is constantly trying to particularize answers to the philosophic questions: "What is man worth?" and "How does man find happiness?"

When I meet a new face on the Edge, I instinctively ask myself: "What has happened to her will? Why is she so dependent on a crisis telephone call?" And I wonder if there is any validity to the old saying: "Where there's a will there's a way." I wonder if Christianity expresses the truth of human nature or whether men are simply victims of blind determinism. So I try to detach myself from the memorized clichés. I try to simply reflect on my own experience. Can I overcome my own moments of depression by sheer force of will? Am I not subject to periods of emotional distress, however light and irrelevant, which just have to be endured. If the author of the *Imitation of Christ* thought faults could be systematically rooted out, this is not true with basic emotional weaknesses. And yet because I experience moments of personal distress over which I have little power, this does not mean I am the victim of social determinism. I experience the radical capacity to ride-out emotional slumps. I experience the radical power to change my opinions when new evidence is put before me. Though tied down by a personality conditioned heavily by heredity, environment and a history of past choices, I experience some freedom to overcome depression.

Yet it would be a mistake for me to judge others by my own experience of psychological freedom. People on the Edge have to be taken as they are. Many of them have little freedom and are not ready for any commitment. When a severely disturbed child meows like a cat and laps up milk, a therapist may have to play cat for a while. Likewise one who would wish to preach the Good News of Christ on the Edge may first have to play "cat" before playing apostle. Those depressed enough to give up on themselves but not neurotic enough to be committed need the help of the People of God. They are the "biblical sick" who "need a physician." And those of us who experience a little more happiness can't simply be content to tell Burt and Ron to "grow up." Any approach to the emotionally infantile must be tempered with the realization there will probably be relapses. And I'm sure Christ realized the tendency towards repeated failure when he admonishes a person to "sin no more." In telling a person not to sin, Christ was not simply moralizing but assuring that individual that he had the radical capacity to liberate himself from demonic forces. While the parent or catechist is not necessarily a trained psychologist or social worker, he or she is one who must stand for hope in the future. Regardless whether one uses the Baltimore Catechism or the latest product of the Biblical Renaissance, the Christian teacher must convey a conviction that all men have the radical capacity to love and be happy.

DYNAMIC APPROACHES TO TEACHING HIGH SCHOOL RELIGION

Sister M. Michael Doherty, I.H.M., Ph.D.

"Smugness in teaching and boredom in learning must be eliminated if youth are to be prepared to cope with the challenges they are about to face. The so-called knowledge explosion and the driving hunger for freedom are among the pressing factors that require other than a textbook for teaching, and especially for the teaching of religion in the post-Vatican II era."

Catechetics in America have come a long way and have a long way to go. In recent years many observant teachers have voiced dissatisfaction with the approaches and methods of teaching religion to teenagers. There is no easy solution; but any viable solution must appreciate the hopes, frustrations and psychology of modern youth.

The author's long experience and research convinced her that new and revolutionary approaches are needed to integrate and correlate the religion course into the total curriculum and to give the student ways and means of becoming involved—and of making his religion personally relevant. Her pioneering study invites teachers to turn the religion classroom into a laboratory: where the student can actively participate and cooperate, where the textbook is no longer the sole or the main method of communication. Her approach and open-ended, adaptable programs open up a new vista of opportunity.

This practical work gets down from theory to practice: it does not underrate the difficulties of adjustments on the part of some teachers; neither does it offer a catechetical panacea. It gives high school and C.C.D. teachers a workable and detailed blueprint which can make the teaching of religion a more challenging, interesting and fruitful vocation.

Cloth: $6.95
Paper: $2.95

EXPLORING VATICAN 2: *Christian Living Today and Tomorrow*
Raymond B. Fullam, S.J.
Exploring Vatican 2 is unlike any other book on the market. It is not another commentary on the Council. The documents themselves do most of the talking. For classroom use this means that assigned readings can be made on the basis of a central vital theme and personal and local applications of the conciliar message can be easily handled in a dialogue situation.

"Those conducting CCD Adult Religious Education courses can profit immensely from the selections arranged in such an enriching thematic sequence." *Rev. William J. Tobin, America*

$2.95 ppr.; $6.95 cl.

POVERTY: SIGN OF OUR TIMES
Aloysius Schwartz
The author of THE STARVED AND THE SILENT makes an impassioned plea on behalf of the poor of the world and calls upon all to a renewal of the spirit and practice of the virtue of poverty as He preached it. A 16 page portfolio of photos is included.

$4.95

PRESENTING CHRIST
Sr. Maria de la Cruz Aymes, H.H.S.
Co-author of *On Our Way* series crystallizes best CCD thinking on critical catechetical problems.

$1.50 ppr.

CHALLENGES OF LIFE
Ignace Lepp

This provactive and thoughtful study of man as he is today is based on the data of scientific experience.

The great themes which occur again and again in modern art and literature are illumnatingly presented. Adventure and risk, freedom and responsibility, the meaning of vocation, the call to growth, the need to keep responsive and openminded toward life, all these are discussed vigorously and clearly.

The author boldly faces up to the basic question of the very possibility of making a free choice, of being committed. Is man merely conditioned and determined? Can he raise above his situation whilst yet remaining in it? Is all this what can be said about sin, about fear, unrest, anxiety?

"This is a book that offers an intense insightful vision of life as an unending series of challenges by which man must grope his way toward God. It manages to communicate hope and enthusiasm for living, as well as the spiritual stimulation of listening to a truly wise, sensitive and optimistic human being . . . a rare piece of writing that has our unreserved recommendation." *The Register*

Book Club of the Month Selection—Sister's Book League, Thomas More Assoc.

$4.95